EYES FOR HAITI

Christian Love in Action

EYES FOR HAITI

Christian Love in Action

By Hal H. Crosswell Jr., MD
Edited by Arlene Andrews

South Carolina United Methodist Advocate Press

South Carolina United Methodist Advocate Press, Columbia, South Carolina

Copyright © 2024 by South Carolina United Methodist Advocate Press

Scripture quotation marked (KJV) is taken from the King James Bible (public domain).

All rights reserved. No part of this book may be reproduced or transmitted in any form or by any means, electronic or mechanical, including photocopying, recording or by any information storage and retrieval system, without permission in writing from the Publisher.

First published in the United States of America in 2024
by the South Carolina United Methodist Advocate Press.

Library of Congress Cataloging-in-Publication Data
Eyes for Haiti
p. cm.

Cover photo and all interior photos courtesy of Dr. Hal Crosswell.
Cover design by Anne Crosswell.

ISBN 979-8-9883575-8-2

Table of Contents

Foreword vii
Chapter 1: The Beginning 1
Chapter 2: Haiti: The Country and Its People 11
Chapter 3: The Eye Teams Begin 15
Chapter 4: A New Generator for the Clinic 43
Chapter 5: A "Miracle" at the Clinic 47
Chapter 6: Cuban Eye Doctors 49
Chapter 7: A New Organ for the Methodist Church 53
Chapter 8: Help from the French 55
Chapter 9: Te Madeline 57
Chapter 10: A Lady Named Catherine 61
Chapter 11: A New Sound System for the Methodist Church 63
Chapter 12: Lyse 65
Chapter 13: God Knows Our Every Need 69
Chapter 14: The Last Surgery Case 71
Chapter 15: Predestination or Coincidence 74
Chapter 16: A New Methodist Church for Despagne 79
Chapter 17: Crick 81
Chapter 18: The Earthquake of 2010 85
Chapter 19: The Present and the Planned Future 93
How to Help 97
About the Author 99

Foreword

This book is dedicated to all the volunteers working through United Methodists Volunteers in Mission and the Methodist Church of Haiti, all who have demonstrated Christian love in action to make this program possible.

It should be noted that UMVIM came to be because of the efforts of Dr. Michael C. Watson, and without this organization, this program would never have happened.

As coordinator of ophthalmology services in the Caribbean region for UMVIM for more than fifty years, God has given me the opportunity to be associated with some of the most talented and dedicated Christians in the world, who include ophthalmologists, optometrists, dentists, nurses, pharmacists, pharmaceutical representatives, opticians, biomedical technicians, construction personnel, electrical engineers, ministers and many wonderful lay people, all of whom helped to make this program so successful.

Also a blessing is that my wife, Kathy, an ophthalmic surgical nurse, was equally as passionate about the program and traveled with me to work on all teams.

This program would not have been possible without the generous contributions of surgical supplies and medications by many of the pharmaceutical companies.

Generous contributions by many churches and individuals, especially from Shandon United Methodist Church in Columbia, South Carolina, have enabled us to continue this program for the last fifty years to provide much-needed eye care for the people with visual problems in the Jérémie region of Haiti.

Because of this program with its many volunteers and supporters, thousands of Haitians have been given the gift of sight.

"And the King shall answer and say unto them, Verily I say unto you, inasmuch as ye have done it unto one of the least of these my brethren, ye have done it unto me" (Matthew 25:40 KJV).

We have all been given different talents by God, and if we use them to help those who are in need, we can certainly help to make this world a better place.

—Dr. Hal Crosswell Jr., May 2024

Dr. Hal Crosswell with one of his favorite patients.

Chapter 1

The Beginning

In November 1968, I received a telephone call from Dr. Michael C. Watson, a family practitioner in Bamberg, South Carolina, and founder of the United Methodist Volunteers in Mission program. He asked if I would agree to meet with him at Trenholm Road United Methodist Church in Columbia to discuss my involvement in a volunteer medical program.

At that time, Mike was serving as medical advisor for United Methodist Committee on Overseas Relief. Mike had received a call from the chief executive of the United Methodist Committee on Overseas Relief, telling him they had received a request for medical assistance from Anguilla, a small island in the Caribbean, as there was no physician on the island at that time. I learned that Anguilla was a small island in the Caribbean Sea's Leeward Islands. It is a British overseas territory with a population of approximately fifteen thousand people of both Irish and African descent. The island itself is approximately thirty-five square miles measuring three miles in width and seven miles in length. The principal industry on the island was the manufacture of salt from seawater and fishing for lobster. Many of the younger inhabitants would leave the island for employment and send money back to their families.

At the meeting with Mike, I learned that several general practitioners from South Carolina were already providing short-term medical care for the people of Anguilla. These doctors had noted a high incidence of eye disease, including cataracts and glaucoma, with no eye care available. Mike asked if I would agree to recruit ophthalmologists to help with this situation. I was also asked to serve as coordinator for ophthalmological services in the Caribbean for what was to become the United Methodist Volunteers in Mission program. I agreed to serve in this position with plans to organize eye teams to help deliver eye care to the people on the island.

Eye teams were organized with plans for each team to be there for two weeks to provide eye care for the people. Arrangements were made to accommodate the teams at Lloyd's Guesthouse, which was located near the hospital in The Valley section of the island. A small hospital was in this region where we were able to set up a small room for eye exams. There was one small operating room, which we used for surgery. There was no air conditioning, with all areas open to the air, which led to uninvited guests in the operating room at times. It was necessary for each ophthalmologist to bring his own surgery instruments with him.

As there was a high incidence of cataracts in the population, hundreds of cataract operations were performed by these teams during the time of this program, in addition to procedures for pterygium and eyelid problems. This program continued until 1974, when the British government began providing medical care for the people there. It is important to note that most of the ophthalmologists who participated in this program volunteered for more than one visit.

During my first visit to Anguilla, I met with the British Commissioner Arthur C. Watson as well as Deputy Commissioner James Campbell. Over time, I met with some of the Anguilla officials, including Mr. Webb (chairman of Counsel), John Webster (secretary of Counsel), and the Reverend Carty (member of Counsel). Commissioner Watson expressed deep appreciation to the South Carolina Conference of The United Methodist Church for providing this much-needed service to the island.

Betty Campbell, wife of Deputy British Commissioner Jim Campbell, had worked as an eye, ear, nose, and throat nurse in England and volunteered her assistance to our teams while we were working there. Her assistance was vital to the success of this program.

Prior to our first visit there, a visual screening team from the University of Waterloo School of Optometry visited Anguilla for several weeks for the purpose of refracting and giving eyeglasses. They were very helpful in the screening of patients with the referral to us for treatment and surgery. I corresponded with Dr. Edward J. Fisher, who was director there, and thanked him for their work as they were so beneficial to our program there. As a side note, we became very good friends with Betty and Jim Campbell, which has continued over the years.

The ophthalmologists who participated in the Anguilla program were as follows:

Shepard N. Dunn, MD—Columbia, South Carolina
Edward D. Hopkins, MD—Columbia, South Carolina
G. Lynn Derrick, MD—Columbia, South Carolina
Don J. Jackson, MD—Columbia, South Carolina
Ronald A. Lanford, MD—Spartanburg, South Carolina
William M. Rowlett, MD—Hopkinsville, Kentucky
Hal H. Crosswell Jr. MD—Columbia, South Carolina

In October 1971, Mike Watson contacted me and Dr. Jennings "Jinx" Owens, a surgeon from Bennettsville, South Carolina, and asked if we would agree to travel to Haiti to meet with the bishop of the Methodist Church of Haiti regarding proposed construction of a medical facility in Jérémie. Mike had received a request from the Methodist Church of Haiti for medical assistance through the United Methodist Committee on Overseas Relief. Previously, Mike—accompanied by agricultural engineer Joe Cal Watson and the Reverend George Strait—had visited the Jérémie area and had proposed construction of a medical facility. Mike and Dr. Marion Dwight along with Rev. Strait had conducted a tetanus immunization program there in 1970.

Dr. Owens and I both had been working in Anguilla, and following our work there, we flew from Santo Domingo, Puerto Rico, to Port-au-Prince, Haiti. Upon our arrival, we were met by the Reverend Alain Rocourt, bishop of the Methodist Church of Haiti. At that time, Haiti was under the rule of the president for life, François "Papa Doc" Duvalier, who was a ruthless dictator. Although we both had valid United States passports, we were surprised to learn we must have a visa to travel in the country.

An appointment had been made by Bishop Rocourt for us to meet with Minister of Health Dr. Alex Theard to discuss our purpose for being there and to obtain a photo identification visa, which would allow us to travel to Jérémie. Dr. Theard was very cordial and was enthusiastically in favor of our proposed work in Jérémie. At the completion of the meeting, he pledged the government's full support in this project. Later that evening, Bishop and

Mrs. Rocourt hosted a dinner at their home, which included several local ophthalmologists and physicians including Dr. George Hudicourt and Dr. Jean Claude DesMangles, both of whom were ophthalmologists in Port-au-Prince. Both would play a vital role in the development of the eye program in Jérémie. This was certainly a most enjoyable and informative evening for all of us. We were then taken to the Plaza Hotel, where reservations had been made for us for our overnight stay.

The following morning, we traveled to Jérémie, which is located approximately 125 miles southwest of Port-au-Prince. As the roads were very bad and unpredictable, the only way to travel was by air or by sea. There was no local air service, so arrangements were made for us to fly with the Haitian Air Force. We were taken to a small government airport, where we boarded an old C-47 aircraft for our journey to Jérémie. I was familiar with this aircraft from my days in the United States Air Force and always knew it to be very reliable. It so happened that the pilot was a Colonel Rocourt, who was a relative of Bishop Rocourt.

Following takeoff, we flew over the beautiful Haitian countryside with a stop at the small town of Les Cayes. As the plane descended for landing, I attempted to see the landing strip through the small window, but there was none, which was concerning to both Jinx and myself. Shortly thereafter, we were bumping along a rugged strip in a sugarcane field. We finally came to a stop near an old shed, which turned out to be the airport.

After some items were unloaded from the plane, we took off and headed for Jérémie. Our flight from Les Cayes took us across a high mountain range. As the plane descended near Jérémie, we were able to see a small landing strip on the side of a hill near the ocean. After a successful landing and deplaning, we could see that this facility, although somewhat primitive, was better than what we had encountered at Les Cayes.

We were met at the airport by Richard Challendes, who was director of the Methodist Rural Rehabilitation project at Gebeau. Richard was a volunteer from Switzerland working with the Methodist Church of Haiti. At this time, the project was supported by not only the Methodist Church of Haiti but also the Methodist Church of England, Switzerland, and France.

We were taken to the Methodist guesthouse to be housed during our stay. Pastor Edward Holmes, a Methodist missionary from England who was serving as superintendent of the Jérémie district, was not there at the time

Above, the passenger bus for Jérémie.

of our visit. In accordance with the instructions we had received from the minister of Health, we proceeded to the small government military outpost to check in with the authorities. It was necessary for us to do this every day while we were there so they could account for our whereabouts. This was Duvalier's way of keeping up with all outsiders who were in the country.

Jérémie is located on the southwest peninsula of Haiti. It is the capital of the Grande Anse region and relatively isolated from the remainder of Haiti. The city is located on the shores of the Gulf of Gonave surrounded by fertile green mountains with the Grande Anse River flowing into the sea nearby. The Grande Anse region is home to more than four hundred thousand people.

Jérémie was founded in 1756 and is also known as the "City of Poets" because of the large number of writers and poets who were born there, including Etzer Vilaire, Émile Roumer, and Gen. Thomas-Alexander Dumas (father of Alexander Dumas). At one time, it was one of the wealthiest cities in Haiti, producing cocoa, sugarcane, bananas, and mangoes. Although this was true in the past, it is certainly not the case now. In 1964, the port of Jérémie was closed by Duvalier, and many of its inhabitants were killed because they opposed his regime.

In driving about the city, poverty was evident everywhere. Still you could not help but notice the old French-style architecture and the "gingerbread houses," which were so unique and beautiful.

Above and below Jérémie is located approximately 125 miles southwest of Port-au-Prince.

We proceeded to the Methodist Rural Rehabilitation project at Gebeau, which was located just across the Grande-Anse River on the outskirts of Jérémie. This project is a multifaceted program dealing with the social needs of people in that region. It was begun in 1967 by the Rev. Rocourt, who was then the superintendent of the Jérémie district. At that time, the project was actively involved in agriculture, home economics, auto repair, woodworking, a

The marketplace in Jérémie.

A small fishing village near Jérémie.

midwife training program, and a medical-tuberculosis clinic.

The medical clinic was a small wooden structure that appeared to be approximately ten-by-twelve-feet in size with little equipment and with less medicine than you would expect to find in one's home medicine cabinet. We were told thousands of patients would come seeking treatment, but many

The "Gingerbread House" in Jérémie.

times no medicines were available. We certainly agreed with Dr. Watson that a new clinic was necessary to serve the needs of the people in that region.

On the following day, we visited Hospital St. Antoine, which is a small government hospital with approximately one hundred beds. Both the wards and the operating room were open-air with no air conditioning. There we met with Dr. Jean Martineau, who was a surgeon and director of the hospital. After a tour that included the one operating room and the separate male and female wards, we discussed the possibility of developing a medical and eye clinic at the Methodist project. He pledged his assistance and cooperation, including allowing us to use the operating room for our eye surgery. He in-

The old gate in Jérémie.

dicated that there were many people in the region who suffered with vision loss from cataracts and other diseases.

We next visited the pediatric ward, where we found several children hospitalized suffering with a condition called kwashiorkor, caused by malnutrition and protein deficiency. All the children were in a terminal state because of this condition. It was so sad to see these children being held by their mothers with nothing we could do to help.

Some time later, to help prevent problems related to food insufficiency, an agricultural program was developed at Gebeau by Joe Cal Watson, from Ridge Springs, South Carolina, who had a degree in agricultural engineering from Clemson University. This program educates the people about how to grow crops that are high in protein. Over the years we have been visiting Jérémie, we have noticed a dramatic decrease in the number of children with this condition. But on that first visit, it was obvious the people were suffering.

During our stay in Jérémie, the weather was very wet and rainy. Fortunately, on the day we were scheduled to depart, the skies cleared. We were able to fly back to Port-au-Prince with the Haitian Air Force.

Upon our return to the United States, we reported to Dr. Mike Watson and the UMVIM committee that we would certainly agree with the plans to construct a new medical-TB clinic that would also include an eye and dental section.

The road in front of the clinic was rustic yet beautiful.

Construction teams from the South Carolina and the Western North Carolina conferences of The United Methodist Church then traveled to Jérémie to construct the new clinics. Completed in 1973, they enabled short-term volunteer medical, dental, and eye teams to begin their work there.

The construction was led by the Reverend Needham Williamson, coordinator of overseas construction projects for the South Carolina Conference Board of Missions, and the Reverend Joe Irvin from the North Carolina Conference of The United Methodist Church.

Chapter 2

Haiti: The Country and Its People

The name "Haiti" is derived from the indigenous Arawak Indian name that means "Land of High Mountains." It was also given a nickname by the French, "Pearl of the Antilles," which appears on all the vehicle license plates in that country today. It is interesting to note that after the Haitian Revolution, the colonial name of the country—St. Domingue, which was the name given to the country by the French—was changed to Haiti.

Haiti is a beautiful country, although there is poverty everywhere. It is here that one will see beauty and poverty alongside each other. The people are warm, friendly, and resilient. Although they face adversity almost every day, they never complain. They all exhibit hope with a beautiful smile on their faces.

The culture of Haiti is a combination of African, French, and West Indian. Haitian Creole and French are the official languages of the country, with most schools teaching in French. In the past, the language was a social divider with the poor speaking primarily Creole while the wealthy and educated spoke French.

Haiti was a colony of France from 1625 to 1804, during which time it was one of the wealthiest colonies of France, as it was the world's leading producer of coffee and sugar during the eighteenth century. The Haitian Revolution began in 1791 and ended in 1804 when the slave army, led by the slave generals, defeated the French. Independence was proclaimed on January 1, 1804. Thus Haiti became the second country in the Western Hemisphere to win freedom from colonial rule, with the first being the

"Haiti" means means "Land of High Mountains" in indigenous Arawak Indian.

United States of America. The Haitian Revolution is also what forced Napoleon Bonaparte, in 1803, to sell the Louisiana territory to the United States.

Another important part of the history of Haiti is the occupation of the country by the United States Marines from 1915 to 1934. This was brought about by the assassination of the president of Haiti in 1915. The resulting chaos prompted United States President Woodrow Wilson, based on the Monroe Doctrine, to send in the Marines to restore stability and order to the country.

Since becoming an independent country, Haiti has been plagued with political instability. This, coupled with social and economic problems that have been magnified by natural disasters, has led to a state of chronic poverty. Many of the people live without electricity or running water, particularly in the countryside. Many depend on the rivers as a source of water. Hunger, starvation, and diseases are prevalent and take their toll on the population every day. The life expectancy of the average person is sixty-three years. Good medical care is available, but the number of health-care providers is far less than in other countries. It is estimated there are only about 0.23 doctors per one thousand people, whereas in the United States there are 2.6 doctors per one thousand people.

The view of Jérémie from the road leading to the town.

The Jérémie marketplace.

Haiti now has a population of more than eleven million people living in an area approximately one-third the size of South Carolina, which makes it one of the most densely populated countries in the Western Hemisphere. It is the first Black republic in the Western hemisphere, and it also bears the distinction of being the poorest nation in Latin America and the Caribbean. The major portion of the economy is from agriculture. Most of the people are peasants who live a very simple lifestyle, inhabiting a small plot of land that they either own or rent. On this land they grow fruits such as bananas, mango, and papaya or vegetables such as sweet potatoes, carrots, and cabbage. These they sell on the street or in the marketplace. The unemployment rate is approximately sixty percent. The average income is approximately $130 a month, or five dollars a day. Many of those who work are considered underemployed, which means they do not make enough to provide for themselves or their families.

Only approximately sixty percent of the population is literate. Although education is compulsory for children ages six through twelve, all the children do not attend school because of lack of facilities and staff. Many of the children attend schools provided by religious groups and churches, which are present throughout the country.

Roman Catholicism is the major religion of the people, with approximately sixty-five percent of the population claiming to be Catholic. Twenty-five percent of the population claims to be Protestant, which includes Methodist, Lutheran, Episcopalian, Presbyterian, and Baptist. The Methodists were the first Protestants allowed to come into Haiti, which occurred in the early nineteenth century. It is said a small number of people, primarily Catholic, combine a part of their religion with the practice of Vodou. Vodou is an intriguing spiritual practice that incorporates ceremonies with song, dances, and fellowship. The Vodou gods are derived from West African religions.

For most of the Haitian people, life is very difficult. However, they face each day with hope and faith. One of the popular Creole proverbs used by the people is "Dèyè mòn gen mòn," which translates to, "Beyond every mountain, there is another mountain." Yet they remain positive and resilient, with hope on their faces every day.

One of my favorite prayers denotes the strong faith of the Haitian people. It comes from *God Is No Stranger*, a collection of prayers used by the Haitian people and written by Sandra L. Burdick and Elizabeth Turnbull.

The prayer is as follows:

"Lord, if we are alive in spite of hurricanes, hunger, and sickness, we should say, 'Thank you, Lord.' We must be here for a purpose. Amen."

Chapter 3

The Eye Teams Begin

After considerable planning and preparation by the United Methodist Volunteers in Mission Committee, in conjunction with the Methodist Church of Haiti, the eye program began in Jérémie, Haiti, in 1974.

The first eye teams were scheduled at two-week intervals beginning March 31, 1974, and ending June 16, 1974. We decided that the ophthalmologist and optometrist with the other members of their eye team would travel to Jérémie at their own expense. This ensured that all donated funds would be used for patient care.

Preparation for this program began some two years earlier by initiating procurement of necessary equipment and supplies for the eye clinic. This was all made possible through generous donations by churches, civic clubs, individuals, and pharmaceutical companies. These companies included Alcon Laboratories; Allergan; Burroughs Wellcome Fund; Lederle; Eli Lilly and Company; Merck Sharp and Dohme; Parke-Davis and Company; Persōn & Covey Inc.; Pfizer Laboratories; Roche Laboratories; Schering Corporation; The Upjohn Company; Wyeth Laboratories; Smith, Miller and Patch; Novartis; Santen; Sonomed; Bausch + Lomb; Lumenis; Johnson & Johnson; and Ethicon. Without the very generous donations of medicines and supplies by these companies, this program would certainly have not been possible.

The equipment needed to set up a complete eye examination room was purchased with donations that had been given over the past year. A very special donation was given by Mrs. Sara-Ellen Ringley to honor the memory of

The Methodist Guesthouse (also known as the "Jérémie Hilton").

Hospital St. Antoine

her grandfather, Dr. Harry Wright McPherson, who was a Methodist minister.

All teams were required to register and obtain clearance from the minister of Health prior to being able to travel to Haiti and work at the clinic in Jérémie. This required that we submit three passport photos; three copies of one's curriculum vitae; and three copies of one's diploma from medical school, optometry school, or nursing school, whichever was appropriate. This

Above and below: the Jérémie airport.

information was due three months prior to the scheduled arrival date. All team members were requested to check with their local health departments regarding required immunizations for travel to Haiti. All team members were also advised to take vitamin B1 (thiamine) one hundred milligrams daily beginning five days prior to departure, which worked well as a mosquito repellant. Aralen (chloroquine phosphate) was also advised to be taken orally to help prevent malaria.

A team travels by road to Jérémie.

The early years set the schedule for arriving teams that is still basically followed today. The teams traveled by air to the Toussaint Louverture International Airport in Port-au-Prince. There they would be met by a representative from the Methodist Church of Haiti. In the early years of this program, the teams would be housed at either The La Plaza Hotel or The Coconut Villa Hotel, as it was not possible to travel on the same day. Then in the early 1980s, a Methodist guesthouse was begun for the purpose of housing all teams coming to Haiti.

It was not uncommon for Bishop Alain Rocourt or Dr. George Hudicourt to invite eye teams to their homes for dinner. The following morning, teams would be picked up and transported to the local Guy Malary Airport, which is located approximately two kilometers from the international airport. There they would board a small aircraft to travel to Jérémie, which is approximately 125 kilometers from Port-au-Prince.

There are three ways to travel to Jérémie: by boat, land vehicle, or air. Air travel is the most convenient and preferred. There have been several airlines available for local travel, including Air Haiti, Carribinair, Sunrise and MAF (Mission Aviation Fellowship) with only the final two in operation at the time of this writing.

In the early years of this program, our eye team at times traveled to Jérémie by land vehicle, which took us approximately eight hours because of the primitive road conditions between Les Cayes and Jérémie. The road was very narrow and rocky as it curved through the mountains. It would require that you pull over when meeting another vehicle as only one can pass at a time. There are several rivers to be crossed along that journey with no bridges. Fortunately, the water was low, so there was no problem driving through the river to the other side. Although the journey was difficult, it was certainly worth it to be able to see the beautiful countryside along the way.

But air travel was faster and easier. The flight from Port-au-Prince to Jérémie originates at the Guy Malary Airport, which is near the international airport and in fact uses the same runway. The flight takes approximately one hour and takes you over the coastline with the mountains in the background. It also flies over many small islands, some of which are inhabited as evidenced by small structures with thatch roofs with small boats nearby.

As the plane approaches Jérémie, one can see the town spread along the coast with the Grande-Anse River emptying into the ocean nearby. The small airport can be seen with its white caliche runway.

After landing, the plane taxis up to a small brightly painted building with a flagpole out front flying the Haitian flag.

The arriving team is then usually met by a representative of the Methodist Church in Jérémie to transport the team and their baggage with either pickup trucks or four-wheel drive vehicles from the airport to the Methodist

Travel by road involved crossing many rivers—with no bridges.

The road was very narrow and rocky as it curved through the mountains.

Guesthouse in town, a distance of several miles. The road follows the coastline and is unpaved with many ruts and multiple potholes. As you ride along, you see many home sites with houses made of plaster and sticks surrounded by palm and banana trees. The roofs are usually made of thatch or palm trees. Usually, people travel along the road on foot, riding a donkey, or sometimes on a motorbike.

Upon arriving in the town, teams travel up the hill passing the government's Hospital Saint-Antoine en route to the parsonage or guesthouse. In the beginning years of this program, teams were housed and fed at the parsonage of Pastor Edward Holmes, who was the superintendent of the Jérémie District of the Methodist Church of Haiti. The adjacent guesthouse was not complete until 1979.

During the years the teams stayed at the home of Pastor Holmes, they were well cared for not only by Pastor Holmes but also by his wonderful housekeeper and cook, Lytane. Beginning in 1979, the visiting teams then enjoyed room and board at the Methodist Guesthouse, which was also called the "Jérémie Hilton" by many of the team members. The guesthouse was large and spacious with approximately six large bedrooms, which contained as many beds as possible for the visiting teams. There were two bathrooms upstairs and one downstairs but no hot water. Most team members will always remember those wonderful cold showers. There was a staff

Jérémie by the sea.

of four ladies who prepared wonderful Haitian meals for each of the teams. Pastor Holmes was reassigned to the Cap Haitian District at that time and was replaced by Pastor Allen Darby and his wife, Betty. Located between these two buildings was the home of the Gebeau Project Director Richard Chalandes and his family.

Over the years we had the privilege of working with many dedicated Christian pastors who served as superintendents of the Jérémie District, all

Downtown Jérémie

Travel by air to Jérémie Airport at Jérémie.

of whom were so important and helpful in the success of this program. In addition to their responsibility for the Gebeau Methodist Project, they were also responsible for thirty-four churches. These Methodist ministers included Pastor Edward Holmes, Pastor Allen Darby, Pastor Moise Isidore, Pastor Alan Kirton, Pastor Raphael Dessieu, Pastor Ralph Denizard, Pastor John Lesly Dorceley, Pastor Christnel Lelievre, Pastor Claudel Zephyr, and Pastor

The airport terminal in Jérémie.

The beach near Jérémie.

Jacob Presumé. Also there have been several directors of the Gebeau Project, which included Richard Challandes, Cecilia and Bill Manness, and Dr. Eric Fabian, who were also important in the success of the program. Further, without the efforts of Pastor Alain Rocourt, who initiated this project and was the bishop when the eye and other clinics were begun, none of this would have ever happened.

The road near the eye clinic.

The road leading out of Jérémie.

The outpatient eye clinic was in the new medical clinic, located on the outskirts of Jérémie in the Rural Rehabilitation Project known as Gebeau. It was approximately three miles from the hospital. The new clinic was constructed by teams from both the South Carolina Conference and the Western North Carolina Conference of the UMC. The South Carolina Conference contributed approximately $20,000 for the construction of this facility.

The eye clinic at Gebeau (Jérémie).

The Reverends Needham R. Williamson and Joe Ervin worked alongside the Haitian workers to build the new clinic.

In the beginning, the eye clinic consisted of a small exam room and minor surgery area in the new just-completed clinic building. There was also a small waiting room for the patients in the clinic. A large circular, thatched-roof, open-air structure was located just in front of the clinic building, where patients would wait when they arrived.

At a meeting with the project director at Gebeau, it was decided that an appointment system would be used for nonemergency patients, whereas those with visual handicap, emergency situations, or those who had traveled a long distance would be seen on the day of their arrival. The people in the Jérémie region were informed about the eye clinic in various ways, including announcements in church. On any day when teams were working at the clinic, it was common to have as many as several hundred people waiting outside. Our Haitian staff screened people seeking care to be sure we would see those with significant eye problems as well as those who had traveled a long distance to get there. It was also decided that there would be a minimal charge of one gourde (approximately twenty cents) for all services, if the patient could afford it, so as not to create a welfare situation. This would also make the patient more responsible for the medications or glasses he might be given.

Very few of the patients could afford that fee, but they were seen regardless of whether they were able to pay. Many would return to pay it later.

We also had an outreach program, which involved mobile eye teams traveling to outlying villages to see patients who could not travel to the clinic for various reasons. Some of the villages included Leon, Bonbon, Moron, Despanges, Abricots, and Roseaux. Patients were examined with portable equipment, with reading glasses given to those whose problem was with near vision. Patients with serious problems such as glaucoma and cataracts were scheduled to be seen at the eye clinic in Jérémie.

From the beginning of this program in 1974—until the construction of the new eye clinic with surgery suite at Gebeau in 1987—surgery was performed at the Hospital Saint-Antoine in Jérémie. This hospital was constructed by the United States Marines during their occupation in the 1930s. Arrangements were made with Dr. John Martineau, who was the surgeon and director of the hospital, for us to use the only operating room two days a week for our surgery.

In addition, we were allowed to use postoperative beds on the wards for overnight stays for patients after surgery. The hospital had two separate wards on either side of the main building—one for males and the other for females. The surgery suite was in the main building along with an office for Dr. Martineau and another small room for the staff. There were also several storage closets, one of which we were allowed to use to store our supplies for surgery. There was no air conditioning and no screens for the windows or doors, so it was all open-air. At times it was so hot that our surgical gloves would fill with perspiration and need to be changed during the procedure. It also was not unusual to encounter various types of insects during a surgical procedure, but they caused no problem other than annoyance.

The city power was unpredictable, and we had no way of knowing when we would lose power. It was not uncommon to need one of the nurses or other assistants to hold a flashlight on the eye to be able to complete the operation. There was no food service, so it was necessary for the family to bring in food for the patient. Although everything was certainly different from back home, we had no cases of postoperative infection (endophthalmitis).

The outside waiting area at the eye clinic.

The waiting room inside the eye clinic.

Some of the teams included a nurse or operating room technician so they could train the Haitian nurses to assist with eye surgery. Over the years, most of the teams learned to speak "medical Creole," which was most helpful in being able to communicate with the patient and Haitian staff during surgical procedures and while working in the clinic.

Two primary sources provided eyeglasses for this program. The Lions

Club donated more than twenty thousand pairs of eyeglasses, and the Methodist "Share A Pair" program produced more than twenty-five thousand pairs of glasses. All of these glasses were collected at the UMVIM warehouse in Leesville, South Carolina, where they were refurbished and catalogued according to their prescription power, then shipped to Haiti. Over the years, it was also necessary for us to purchase many thousands of reading glasses for use in this program. Although surgery was an important part of this program, giving an older person reading glasses so they could see up close to do their work and other duties was just as important and appreciated.

The use of this warehouse was donated by Dr. R. B. "Bud" Antley, an optometrist who not only has served on many eye teams to Haiti but also has volunteered his time for the packaging and shipment of medications and supplies to Jérémie. During the early years of this program, this very important job was performed by Bud along with Dr. James Mitchell, who was a pharmacist in Leesville, South Carolina. Certainly, without the time and effort these two people spent in packaging and shipping medications and supplies to Jérémie, this program would not have been possible.

All the surgery was performed at Hospital Saint-Antoine until 1987. Cataract surgery during that time was performed with the use of magnifying glasses (loupes) worn by the surgeon. The surgery consisted of an extracapsular removal of the lens with no implant, as they were not available to us then.

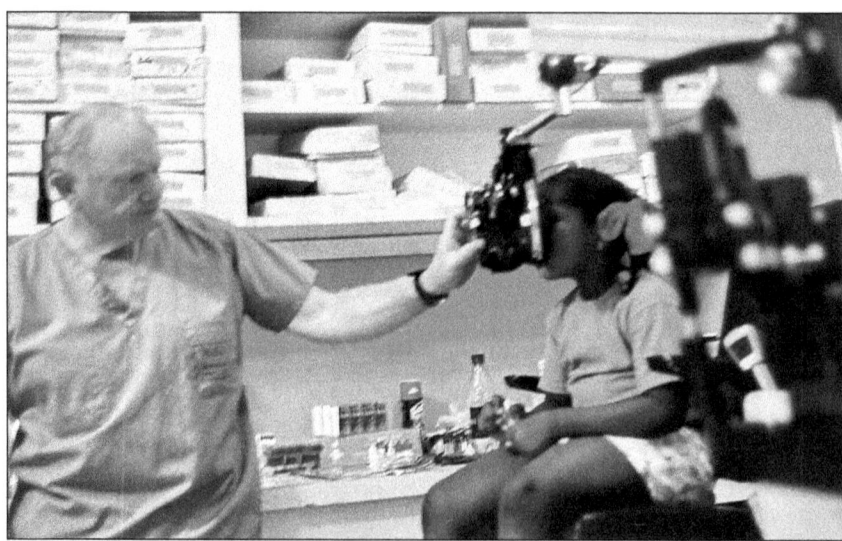

Dr. Antley examines a child.

The building team from Bethany UMC, Summerville, in January 1987.

But in 1987, with the construction of the new eye clinic and surgery suite at Gebeau, we began performing extracapsular cataract surgery using an operating microscope with intraocular lens implantation at the time of the surgery. Some of the first cataract surgeries with lens implantation in Haiti were performed at this clinic. In fact, we learned that the very first surgery of this type in Haiti was performed at our eye clinic in Jérémie.

In January 1987, a construction team from Bethany United Methodist Church in Summerville, South Carolina, led by the Reverend Needham Williamson, traveled to Jérémie for the purpose of enlarging the eye clinic. They built a new surgery suite attached to the medical clinic at the Methodist project at Gebeau. The other members of the team were Tim McConnell, Gillis McAllister, George Keefer, Jackie Rommillat, Martha Jo Rommillat, Linda Rommillat, Ken Willard, Janice Loggins, Joe Stasiukaitis, Steve Vaughn, A. B. Altman, Bob Tryon, Tracey Williamson, and Laurence Williamson. The team worked alongside the Haitian workers to complete this much-needed enlargement of the eye clinic.

The new addition of the clinic and surgery adjacent to each other allowed us to be much more efficient in our care for patients. The addition of an air conditioning unit for the operating room certainly made for a more comfortable surgery for both the patient and the surgeon. Also, a small five-kilowatt generator was added to provide for a more stable power source.

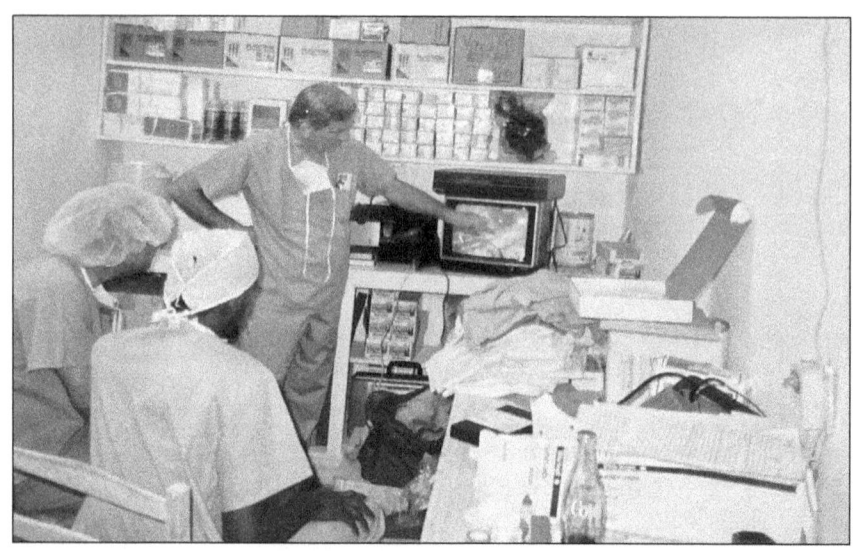

Discussing technique for cataract surgery with Haitian ophthalmologists.

Eye teams were now able to see patients in the clinic and perform surgery at the same location, which was so much more efficient. Patients could have surgery on the same day they were assessed at the clinic. This was particularly beneficial for those who had traveled a long distance to get to the clinic. With the innovation of intraocular lenses to correct the vision after cataract surgery, we were now able to give the patient visual improvement on the same day as surgery. The patients were so appreciative and happy.

Over the next several years, our eye surgical nurses, Kathy and Beth, trained Haitian nurses who worked at the eye clinic in how to assist the surgeon in this new procedure. One of these nurses was Dario Poulemont. We made a video in our operating room in Columbia, South Carolina, demonstrating the details in setting up the operating room for eye surgery, which was very helpful in their training. We also made a video demonstrating each step in the technique of planned extracapsular cataract surgery with intraocular lens implantation, which helped our Haitian ophthalmologists learn this procedure. The language for both videos was in English and Creole thanks to the help of Rose Mae Dumond, who was a student at Columbia College under sponsorship of the UMVIM scholarship program.

In the early years of this program, our eye teams worked in Jérémie for only four to six months, from January to June. Therefore, follow-up care for both surgery cases and for patients with other conditions, such as

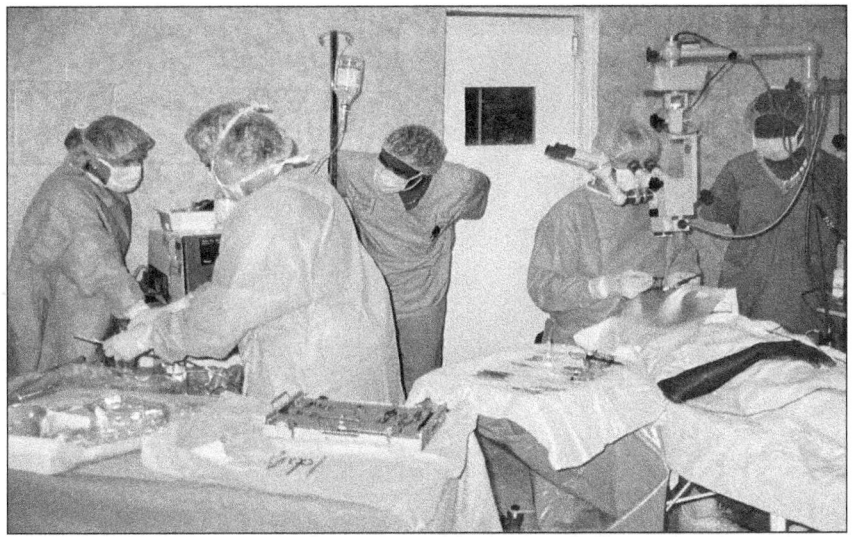

Performing cataract surgery in the eye clinic surgery room.

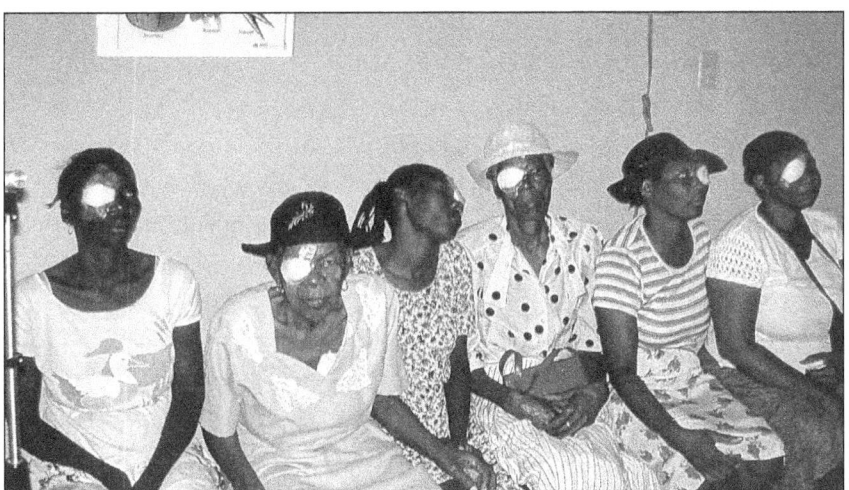

Post-operative patients wait to be examined.

glaucoma, was provided by two ophthalmologists from Port-au-Prince: Dr. Jean Claude Desmangles and Dr. George Hudicourt. These doctors were so involved and instrumental in the development of this program. After we began performing surgery at the eye clinic at Gebeau, Dr. Demangles would often come to Jérémie to work with me and, on several occasions, would bring a young ophthalmologist, Dr. Frantz Large, with him.

Several years later, our team was always joined during our work in Jérémie by Dr. Brigitte Hudicourt, the daughter of Dr. George Hudicourt,

The building team from Shandon UMC, Columbia, led by Lee McDonald, in August 2000.

and Dr. Francoise Rocourt Dennery, the daughter of Bishop Alain Rocourt. Both were so helpful and made the work of our team so much more efficient and enjoyable. In 2007, Dr. Hudicourt and Dr. Dennery brought along with them Dr. Sadrac "Johnny" Marcelus, who was just completing his residency in ophthalmology at the University Hospital in Port-au-Prince. We worked with him in both the clinic and surgery, teaching him some of our techniques. As it turned out, we were all very favorably impressed with his management of patients and surgical skills. Therefore, we offered him a position at the eye clinic to work one week each month. This enabled us to provide year-round care at the clinic even when teams from the United States were not there. This was approved by the superintendent of the Jérémie District of the Methodist Church of Haiti. Johnny has been a part of our clinic staff since that time and continues to provide quality eye care for patients in the Jérémie area.

While the eye clinic was very efficient, the fact that this was the only such facility in the Jérémie region meant large numbers of patients seeking help with their visual problems. It soon became evident that a larger clinic was needed. So in 1998, we began making plans for an expansion to better serve the needs of the people in that region.

After considerable deliberation and consultations, the final plans were to build a new addition to the existing building to include a large waiting room,

Bill Dunn with the electrical team.

The building team from Bethany UMC, Summerville, in January 2001.

receptionist area, two exam lanes, small pharmacy for eye medications, storage room, minor surgery area, and pre-op and post-op room large enough for five beds. We also made plans to remodel the operating room with an addition of a small work room for sterilizers and surgical supplies. As well, we determined a larger generator was needed for power for all the clinics.

The first team to begin preparation and construction for the new eye clinic at Gebeau was led by the Reverend Bruce Palmer in July 2000. With

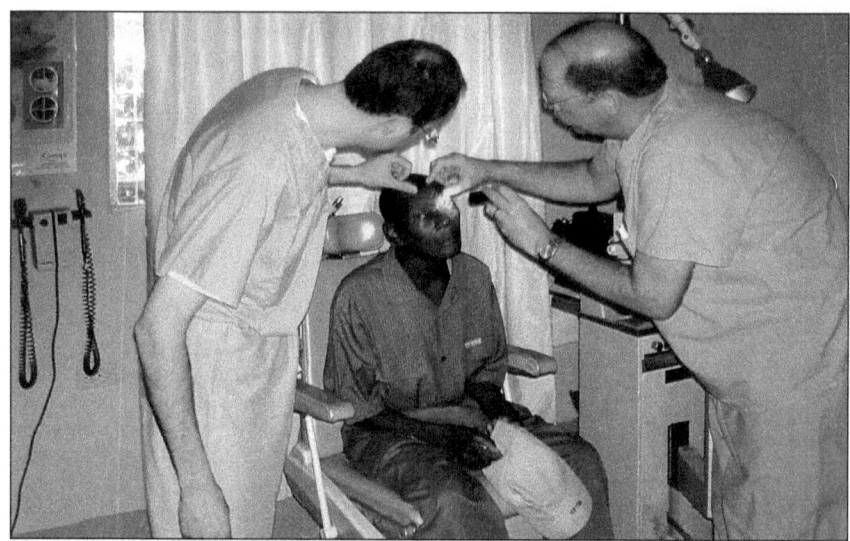

Dr. Finlay and Dr. Gasper examine the eye of a patient.

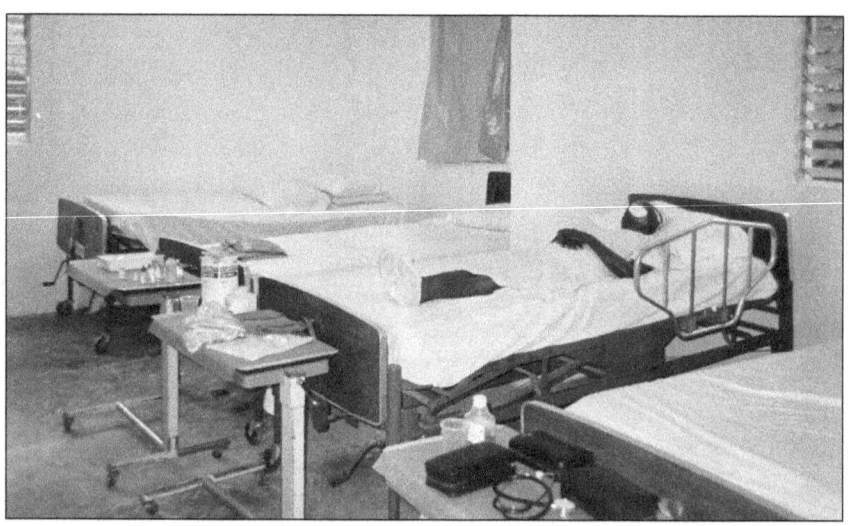

The post-operative recovery area.

Gesner and Bill Dunn, members of that team, demolition of the old eye clinic began. The second team in August 2000 was led by Lee McDonald, with a team comprising all members from Shandon United Methodist Church in Columbia. Their job was to complete the demolition and begin construction with the Haitian workers, which consisted of tying rebar along with mixing and pouring concrete. The team members were Kirk Adams, Michelle Hoffman, Winna Ellis, Cam Treese, Hal French, Frank Kendrick,

The building team from Shandon UMC, Columbia, June 30 to July 8, 2001.

John Taylor, Bruce Mallick, Shelia Lockhart, David Coward, and Sara Adams. We asked the team to be sure there were windows in the examination rooms, which was done.

Electrical teams led by Bill Dunn traveled to Jérémie four times to renovate the entire electrical system at the clinics. They installed new transfer switches and panel boards. In 2001, they were there to help install and connect the new fifty-kilowatt generator into the clinic electrical system. Team members were Homer Stanton, Earl Jeffcoat, Gesner Dunn, Paul Rung, Wilbur Windham, and David Coward.

The third team was from Bethany United Methodist Church in Summerville. Led by Casey Canonge, the team included Chuck Swenson, Frank Zeigler, Linda Roumillat, Jack Roumillat, Joe Stasiukaitis, Phyllis Scheierman, Roanna Payne, Connie Baty, John Stoloff, Ruth Anne Ivey, and Gillis McAllister. It was their job to scrape and sand the cinderblock structure to get it ready for painting, as well as to complete the electrical and plumbing work and to install all doors (including security grates and doors), cabinets, and shelving. Working with their Haitian helpers, they were able to complete all of this during their time in Jérémie.

The new eye clinic and surgery room were now ready for the first eye team, which was arriving the next week.

Our eye team arrived in Port-au-Prince on the same day the team from

The Shandon UMC, above in July 2002, did painting and finishing work at the clinic.

Bethany United Methodist Church returned from Jérémie. We had time to discuss the new addition when we all met at the Methodist Guesthouse in Port-au-Prince and enjoyed an evening meal together. We expressed our sincere appreciation not only for their willingness to travel to Haiti but also for their hard work in completing this much-needed renovation and construction of the new eye clinic and surgery suite.

Roper Hospital in Charleston, South Carolina, donated furniture for the new pre- and post-operative area. Roper had just renovated a part of the hospital that included new beds, tables, and chairs, thereby allowing for their donation of five beds with mattresses, five chairs, and five tables for use in the eye clinic.

Arrangements were made with the help of Congressman Floyd Spence for these items to be transported to Port-au-Prince by the South Carolina Air National Guard, who were scheduled to fly to the Caribbean area on a training mission at that time. The items were packed and put in crates by an UMVIM team prior to their transport to Haiti.

Once they arrived at the airport in Port-au-Prince, they were met by officials of the Methodist Church of Haiti, who then arranged for their transport to Jérémie.

In June 2001, another team from Shandon United Methodist Church traveled to Jérémie to help with the construction and renovation of the medical and dental clinics. The team leaders were Lee McDonald and Ron Berry. The team members were Frank Kendrick, Gesner Dunn, Bill Dunn, Cindy Reid, Glenda McCue, Dan Osborne, Barry Boyle, Mark Cunningham, and Mike Penland.

Another team from Shandon United Methodist Church traveled to Jérémie in July 2002 to complete the finishing work and painting of the clinics. They reported that they applied seventy gallons of white primer and ceiling paint in addition to 105 gallons of green paint to the interior and exterior walls. The team leaders were Bill Dunn and Frank Kendrick. Team members were Carl Primeaux, Lee McDonald, Edwin Martin, Gesner Dunn, Glenda McCue, Jane Hall, Clavis Anderson, and Jim Kitchens.

In 2007, an overnight stay facility was constructed just adjacent to the clinic. It was large enough to accommodate four patients. This facility provides a place to stay overnight for those patients who live a long distance from the clinic. Meals are provided by the clinic staff.

Donations allowed us to purchase a new Zeiss operating microscope with foot controls for focus and magnification, which was placed in the new operating room. We also had an Alcon Legacy 20,000 Phacoemulsification instrument donated, which could be used for both small incision phaco cataract surgery as well as the standard extracapsular technique for cataract surgery. Two new sterilizer units were placed in the surgery work room along with two sets of eye surgery instruments and all medical supplies necessary for eye surgery. All the intraocular lenses that are used for surgery are expensive and were graciously donated by pharmaceutical companies.

A new fifty-kilowatt diesel generator was purchased thanks to a generous donation by two members of the congregation at Shandon United Methodist Church. The generator was transported to Jérémie from Port-au-Prince and was ready for installation when our first eye team arrived in 2001. Bill Dunn, along with his team of Wilbur Windham and Homer Stanton, were in Jérémie preparing for the installation when it arrived. (A section with details regarding the new generator is in Chapter 4 of this book.)

Glaucoma occurs in the Haitian population at a greater incidence than in the United States. The incidence in the general population in Haiti is more than 10 percent, while in the United States it is much lower, around 2 to 3 percent. It is one of the leading causes of irreversible blindness in the world and is often referred to as the silent thief of vision, as there are no early

The eye team with Haitian staff at the eye clinic.

symptoms in most cases. Our clinic is equipped with modern instruments that are used to check the intraocular pressure in all patients who are examined at our clinic. Most cases of glaucoma can be controlled with topical medications if they are available. However, even when the medications are available, there is also a problem with compliance.

In 2013, we were fortunate to have a Selective Laser Trabeculoplasty laser instrument donated by Lumenis Ophthalmic Equipment Company for use in our clinic. It was the first instrument of this kind to be used in the treatment of glaucoma in Haiti. It has been shown to be effective both as a monotherapy and as an additive with topical glaucoma medications. It is very effective in the treatment of patients who are non-compliant. Since we began the use of this instrument, hundreds of patients with glaucoma have been treated, which hopefully has helped to lower the number of blind patients affected by glaucoma.

The most common cause of curable blindness that is seen at the clinic is cataracts. Many of the patients with cataracts had been blind for several years and had their vision restored with cataract surgery. This made for very happy and thankful patients! Since the beginning of this program, thousands of patients have undergone sight-restoring cataract surgery at this clinic.

During the fifty years of this program, there were some years that we were unable to travel to Haiti because of political unrest with associated

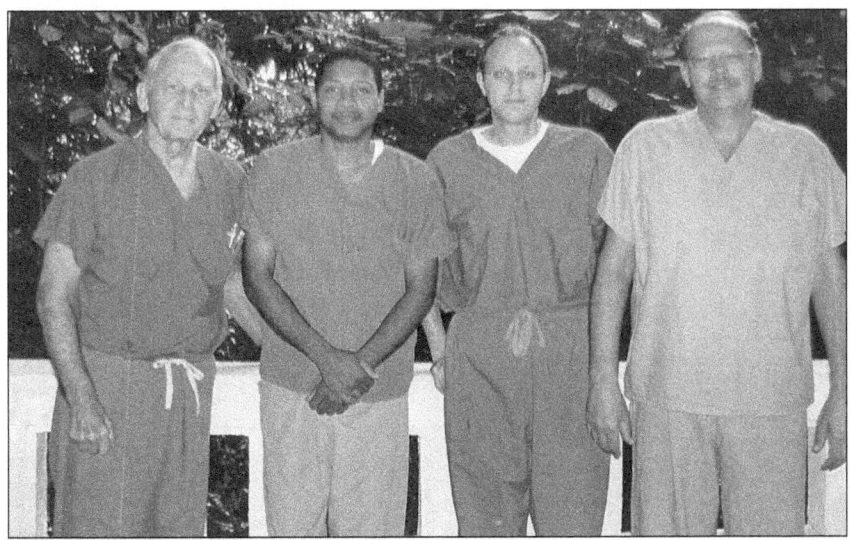

From left are me, Dr. Mike Maingrette, Dr. Finlay, and Dr. Gasper.

violence. Still, we were able to provide quality eye care to many thousands of patients in the Jérémie region. During the years that we were unable to travel to Haiti, members of our Haitian staff were able to provide care. Many of these patients had life-threatening conditions such as glaucoma and cataracts, while others only needed only reading glasses for their close work, such as sewing and reading their Bible.

I have had the privilege to work with so many dedicated Christian eye-care professionals and support individuals who have allowed us to provide quality eye care for the people in the Jérémie region of Haiti for the past fifty years. Without their willingness to volunteer and participate in this program, none of this would have ever been possible. They all truly demonstrated Christian love in action.

Optometrists:
R. B. "Bud" Antley, OD—Batesburg, South Carolina
Greg Bailey, OD—Lexington, South Carolina
James Howard, OD—Seneca, South Carolina

Ophthalmologists:
Edward Darrell Jervey, MD—Greenville, South Carolina
Joe Frank Garner, MD—Charleston, South Carolina
Carl A. Green, MD—Columbia, South Carolina

The eye team at the guesthouse prepares to travel to the eye clinic.

Hunter R. Stokes, MD—Florence, South Carolina
John D. Compton, MD—Greenwood, South Carolina
George H. Jones, MD—Baton Rouge, Louisiana
Von C. Joffrion, MD—Franklinton, Louisiana
Wilbur J. McElroy, MD—Topeka, Kansas
Lowell W. Wilder, MD—Wichita, Kansas
Thomas C. Spoor, MD—Columbia, South Carolina
Quentin P. Hamilton, MD—Southfield, Michigan
Robert E. Livingston III, MD– Newberry, South Carolina
Brian Prater, MD—Maysville, Kentucky
Charles B. Carter, MD—Vancouver, Washington
W. Scott Wilkinson, MD—Clarkston, Michigan
William A. Johnson, MD—Columbia, South Carolina
Thomas M. Leland, MD—Charleston, South Carolina
Alvin W. North, MD—Atlanta, Georgia
Edward C. Mattison, MD—Anderson, South Carolina
Baxter F. McClendon, MD—Charleston, South Carolina
John W. Reed, MD—Winston-Salem, North Carolina
Charles M. Suttonfield, MD—Lynchburg, Virginia
Hal Holland Crosswell III, MD—Columbia, South Carolina
Edward G. Crosswell MD—Columbia, South Carolina

The eye team gathers with Dr. Brigitte Hudicort and Dr. Françoise Rocourt Dennery.

Fulton J. Gasper, MD—Orangeburg, South Carolina
Welbourne A. White, MD—Columbia, South Carolina
Charles D. Finlay, MD—Columbia, South Carolina
H. Felton Cofer, MD—Panama City, Florida
George Hudicourt, MD—Port-au-Prince, Haiti
Jean Claude Desmangles, MD—Port-au-Prince, Haiti
Frantz Large, MD—Port-au-Prince, Haiti
Michael Maingrette, MD—Port-au-Prince, Haiti
Brigitte Hudicourt, MD—Port-au-Prince, Haiti
Françoise Rocourt Dennery, MD—Port-au-Prince, Haiti
Sadrac Marcelus, MD—Port-au-Prince, Haiti
Robert O. Brown. MD—Clemson, South Carolina
Miladis Sintes Jiminez, MD—Cuba
Ana Ariosa Pineda, MD—Cuba
Bernard Martin, MD—Cosqueville, France
Agnes Martin, MD—Cosqueville, France
Phillip Breteau, MD—Cosqueville, France
Hal H. Crosswell Jr., MD—Columbia, South Carolina

Nurses:
Beth Wilkinson, RN—Chapin, South Carolina
Kathryn Crosswell, RN—Columbia, South Carolina

Joan Anastasia, RN—Columbia, South Carolina
Brenda Morgan, RN—Columbia, South Carolina
Cheryl Burgess—Optician

Biomedical Engineers:
James Rawls—Lexington, South Carolina
Tal Morgan—Columbia, South Carolina
Wayne Platteter—North Carolina
Dennis McCutcheon—North Carolina

I led the first eye team to Jérémie in 1974. I think it is important to note that the doctors who followed with eye teams that first year all truly took a leap in faith, not knowing very much about where they were going or the conditions in which they would be working.

These ophthalmologists were Dr. E. Darrell Jervey, Dr. Hunter R. Stokes, Dr Carl A. Green, Dr. Robert E. Livingston, and Dr. Joe Garner. We certainly encountered some bumps in the road, but with all things considered, it was a very successful beginning to this program.

In 2001, Dr. Jervey and his wife, Pat, were instrumental in starting the eye program at the Episcopal Project in Cange, Haiti.

I am very proud that two of my sons, Holland and Edward, both of whom are ophthalmologists, and two of my daughters, Suzanne and Mary Kathryn, were able to participate in this program. My other son, Marcus, wanted to participate but was unable to arrange it with his school schedule. I think that they, along with all who have participated in the Jérémie Eye Program, will echo the fact that working with those who are so much less fortunate is truly life-changing.

I would like to express my sincere gratitude and appreciation to all our team members who traveled with me to Jérémie for so many years. They are all a very dedicated and talented group of individuals who included Beth Wilkinson, RN; Kathryn Crosswell, RN; Cheryl Burgess; Tal Morgan; Dr R. B. "Bud" Antley; Dr. Charles D. Finlay; and Dr. Fulton J. Gasper. I also thank our Haitian friends, Dr. Brigitte Hudicourt and Dr Françoise Rocourt Dennery, both of whom are not only very talented ophthalmologists but also good friends. They were always there to work with us and help with this program.

Chapter 4

A New Generator for the Clinic

From the beginning, electrical power was always a problem for all of the Methodist clinics at Gebeau. Power provided by the city of Jérémie was always unpredictable, with frequent outages and power surges.

For that reason, a small five-kilowatt generator was installed just outside the clinic by the building team from Bethany United Methodist Church in Summerville, South Carolina, while they were there working on the new eye clinic in 1987. With this new source of power we were able to function much better, although it was not ideal. We found we were unable to use all of our equipment in the eye surgery room at one time as it would overload the system. Therefore, we would have to turn off certain pieces of equipment, such as the air conditioner and sterilizer, so the other equipment such as the surgical microscope and phacoemulsification unit would function properly.

In addition, other areas in the clinic were not able to function fully while we were performing surgery. We managed to work with this system for several years, but it was apparent that a larger generator was necessary so other areas of the clinic could function while we were performing surgery.

In 2000, it was proposed to the South Carolina United Methodist Volunteers in Mission board that a fundraiser be initiated to raise the money for a new and more powerful generator for all the Methodist clinics in Jérémie.

One Sunday morning, I was in the back hallway at Shandon United Methodist Church when I was approached by Tom Knox. Tom told me he and his brother Marion would like to help with the purchase of the new

The new generator for the clinic took fifteen men to unload.

generator for the clinic. He then handed me a check for $25,000 and said if that was not enough to let them know.

I was overwhelmed with their generosity. UMVIM-SC was most appreciative of their gift.

With the help of Jim Covington, we contacted Joe Blanchard at Blanchard Equipment in Columbia, South Carolina. Joe agreed to sell us a fifty-kilowatt generator for a reduced price of $18,000, which included his shipping it to Port-au-Prince. When I told Tom and Marion we were able to purchase the generator for less than they had given us, they said for us to use the excess balance to purchase other needed equipment at the clinics. I and the board of UMVIM-SC were very appreciative for the reduced price given to us by Joe Blanchard.

In January 2001, the new generator arrived in Port-au-Prince, Haiti, and was then transported to Jérémie by boat, which took several days. When it arrived at the wharf in Jérémie, it was loaded onto a truck and carried to the site of the Methodist clinics at Gebeau.

Bill Dunn and his team, consisting of Wilbur Windham and Homer Stanton, were in Jérémie several days before our team arrived. However, we were all there when the generator arrived at the clinic area of the project at Gebeau.

A concrete pad had been constructed just behind the clinic where the generator would be placed. It was approximately twelve-by-twelve-feet in

This new generator allowed the clinic to take care of more people needing help.

size with a thickness of ten inches.

The generator arrived on the back of a large open truck. We all were wondering how they would be able to get that large, heavy generator from the truck and onto the concrete pad, which was approximately fifty feet away.

A group of approximately fifteen men had been hired for this job. They had cut trees of varying diameter and stripped them of their limbs. The tailgate of the truck was then lowered to the ground and was at an angle of approximately forty-five degrees. Several ropes were tied to the generator with some to the front and some to the rear. Some of the small trees were then placed on the tailgate adjacent to the generator.

On a given signal, some of the men at the back held it while men at the front were pulling and slowly rolling the huge generator on the trees down the tailgate to the ground. Some of the men would transfer the logs from the back to the front of the generator, while all the others pulled it toward the concrete pad.

When they were close to the pad, trees with increasingly larger diameters were placed like a wedge up the side of the pad. The heavy generator was then pulled up this wedge onto the pad, with some of the men placing smaller trees just in front of the generator as it was rolled across the pad and centered.

We all were amazed and felt like we had watched something comparable to the building of the pyramids.

Bill, Homer, and Wilbur then completed all the wiring and connection to the clinic buildings. A shed was later constructed over the generator for its protection.

Having this source of reliable and uniform power greatly increased the efficiency of the work in not only the eye clinic but also the dental, medical, and tuberculosis clinics.

A big thank you goes to Tom and Marion Knox for their generous gift to make this possible. As well, a big thank you goes to Bill Dunn, Wilbur Windham, and Homer Stanton for all their hard work and expertise in getting the generator working.

This new generator allowed us to take care of more of the people needing our help.

Chapter 5

A "Miracle" at the Clinic

One day while we were busy seeing patients in the clinic, a young teenage girl came in with a complaint of having lost one of her eyes from an accident several years earlier. Fortunately, her remaining eye was normal with twenty-twenty vision.

Examination of the eye that was lost revealed the eyelids to be normal. The eye socket was clean with only a small amount of scarring. We asked both her and her mother if she would like to have an artificial eye for cosmetic purposes, to which she responded in a very positive manner with a big smile.

In the eye clinic, we were fortunate to have a fitting case containing an assortment of ceramic artificial eyes that varied in both size and color. After comparing the color in her remaining eye, we were able to find a good match for the color and size, which fit perfectly.

After inserting the prosthesis, we handed her a mirror so that she could see the results. Both she and her mother were so happy and appreciative.

Shortly thereafter she began screaming that she could see from the new artificial eye! She was running around the clinic screaming, "Thank you, Jesus, I can see again—I can see again!"

I tried to get her to be still long enough for me to cover the good eye so she would realize she could not see from the new artificial eye, but she would not be still long enough for me to do so.

As she ran through the waiting room to the outside area, many of the patients who heard her had gotten down on their knees and were thanking

God for this young girl's apparent cure of her blindness. When she approached the thatched roof gazebo waiting area outside, she continued to scream the same words over and over: "Thank you, Jesus, I can see again!"

This led them all to believe a true miracle had occurred, so many of the patients were on their knees saying a prayer.

Although the young girl's mother seemed to understand what we were saying, I'm not sure we ever convinced that young girl she could not see out of that artificial eye.

It is of interest to note that the following day, many of the patients who we had already seen with blindness from varying causes returned requesting one of the eyes like the young girl had received.

Chapter 6

Cuban Eye Doctors

In 2000, I received an email from Pastor Raphael Dessieu, who was the superintendent of the Jérémie District for the Methodist Church in Haiti.

In his email, Pastor Dessieu told me the government of Haiti had entered into an agreement with the government of Cuba that would allow Cuban doctors to work in certain areas of Haiti, including Jérémie. He went on to say that in the group of doctors from Cuba, there was an ophthalmologist by the name of Dr. Anna Ariosa Pineda, and the Director of Hospital had asked if it would be possible for her to work at the eye clinic at Gebeau while she was in Jérémie. The hospital had no equipment or room for her to work there.

When our team arrived in January 2000, we met Dr. Anna at the clinic. A wonderful friendship developed between her and our team. We were surprised to learn she had no instruments or equipment with her, but as we were well-equipped at the clinic, that was not a problem. She was fluent in Spanish, Creole, and English, which made communication easy.

We, of course, were happy to have her work with us. As she had no ocular instruments or equipment with her, we gave her a set of handheld eye instruments to use while she was there.

After familiarizing her with all the equipment and medications, we all went to work. We were certainly impressed with her overall knowledge of ophthalmology. She demonstrated excellent surgical skills, particularly in cataract surgery. Although she had never performed any cataract surgery with intraocular lens implants, she was eager to learn. We enjoyed working

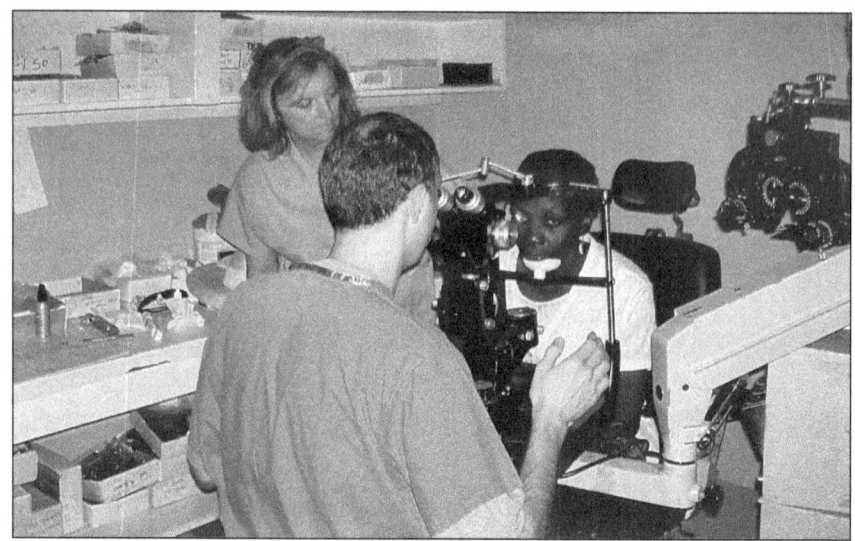

Dr. Finlay and Cheryl work in the clinic with a patient.

with Dr. Anna, as did other teams for the next two years.

In 2003, another ophthalmologist from Cuba arrived—Dr. Meladis Sintes Jiminez. Like Dr. Anna, she was fluent in Spanish, Creole, and English. She, too, was well-trained and possessed excellent surgical skills. As with Dr. Anna, she had performed many cataract surgeries but never any with intraocular lens implants. She, too, had no equipment and no instruments with her, so we presented her with a diagnostic kit. She was most appreciative and happy.

While Dr. Meladis was in Jérémie, there was also a Cuban biomedical engineer who was working at the hospital. When he heard that Tal Morgan, an American biomedical engineer, was at our clinic, he came over for a visit and asked Tal if he could come to the hospital with his instruments to help repair a piece of equipment. So Tal took his instrument case and went along with him to the hospital where they repaired a sterilizer. During the remainder of our visit, Tal helped him repair several more pieces of equipment at the hospital. We certainly enjoyed our association with our Cuban colleagues while our team was there.

Dr. Meladis remained in Jérémie for two years and was a member of the eye clinic staff during her entire time there.

Prior to our departure, the Cuban technician came by to say goodbye to our team. At that time, Tal brought out his tool case and opened it. He then asked the Cuban technician to choose some of the instruments he would need in his work at the hospital and told him he could keep them.

The technician became so emotional and, with tears in his eyes, thanked Tal and expressed his heartfelt appreciation for this kind gesture.

The Cuban eye doctors were surprised to find a group of Americans helping others and not being compensated. In Cuba, they had been taught that Americans were very capitalist, so they did not expect to find us there doing humanitarian work.

We were happy to have been able to educate them about Americans and their generosity.

The Methodist Church in Jérémie received a new electric organ to replace its old pump organ.

Chapter 7

A New Organ for the Methodist Church

The Methodist Church in Jérémie was built in 1850 and is the oldest standing Protestant church in Haiti. Methodism was the first Protestant religion invited into Haiti in 1817, where the official Christian religion of the country was Catholicism beginning in 1697, when it was introduced into Haiti by the French..

In the early years, the Methodist Church in Jérémie held two services on Sunday morning, one in French and the other in Creole. This is now no longer the case, as Creole is now the official language of Haiti, so all services are in Creole.

Our teams would usually worship there on Sunday morning, when people of all ages wearing their best clothes came to the church. Most of the time, all the wooden pews were completely filled with people standing around the inside walls of the church. The children would usually sit along the altar rail at the front of the church. Worshippers who were unable to get into the church would stand around the large windows on the outside.

In the 1970s, the choir director and organist was a man named Benito. His wife was one of the nurses who worked with us in the eye clinic as well as a member of the choir. The area for the choir was always filled with both women and men who had beautiful voices. The majority were usually women. The only organ was an old pump organ. Therefore, most of the hymns sung by the choir were *a cappella*.

When the congregation would sing hymns, Benito would pump the old organ and provide the best music possible. The weather was usually quite warm, and as there was no air conditioning, it was difficult for Benito to pump, play, and direct the choir without becoming overheated. As his energy waned, later in the service the tempo of the hymns would become notably slower.

One of our volunteer ophthalmologists, Dr. Darrell Jervey and his wife, Pat, were attending church in 1975 when they witnessed all of this and felt an urge to do something to help. Upon their return to Greenville, South Carolina, they both raised money from various organizations and friends in order to acquire a new organ for the church.. They purchased a new electric organ that was shipped to Jérémie and installed in the Methodist Church.

Of course, Benito, the minister, the choir, and the entire congregation were overjoyed with this new organ.

I can testify to the fact that the quality and tempo of the music improved dramatically, and Benito was not exhausted at the completion of the service.

Chapter 8

Help from the French

One day in January 1999, I received an international call from a Mr. Ludovic Ravet who identified himself as a Rotarian in Cosqueville, France, in the Normandy region.

Mr. Ravet jokingly told me he was one of the few Frenchmen who liked Americans. He went on to say he had read in the Rotary International magazine about the eye program in Jérémie, Haiti, and my being a Rotarian.

He let me know three ophthalmologists and a nurse in his Rotary club were interested in participating in this program.

After several telephone calls and written correspondence, all was arranged. A team of three ophthalmologists—Dr. Bernard Martin, Dr. Agnes Martin, and Dr. Phillip Breteau—along with a nurse, Mrs. Mary Breteau, would travel to Haiti to work in the eye clinic at Gebeau for two weeks in May 1999.

They traveled to Jérémie and had a very productive time, seeing many patients in the clinic and performing many cataract surgeries. They expressed the fact that they were very impressed with both the eye clinic and staff.

When the schedule was sent out later for the next year, they again volunteered for two weeks in 2000.

The small Methodist Church in the village of Te Madeline.

Chapter 9

Te Madeline

On one Sunday in January 2013, several members of our eye team accompanied Pastor Chrisnel Le Lievre to the small village of Te Madeline in the mountainous countryside outside of Jérémie.

On that day, the pastor would be conducting services at the small Methodist church there. After leaving the main road, we enjoyed a beautiful drive over a narrow, winding, rocky road that led us to the little village of Te Madeline.

The small Methodist Church there was constructed with stucco walls and a thatch roof with large open windows and doors. As we arrived, we could hear the choir singing, accompanied by an accordion.

We entered the church and took our seats on one of the narrow wooden benches near the front. As was the usual case, the church was filled with people dressed in their best clothes with the children sitting on the floor near the front of the church. During the service, both the choir and the congregation sang many hymns accompanied by a young man on the accordion, which lent so much to the music.

Pastor Chrisnel delivered a sermon in Creole regarding the meaning of Communion. At times he would say a few words in English so we would know what the sermon was about. Following the sermon, we all participated in Communion, which consisted of bread and grape juice. It was so meaningful to all of us.

At the beginning of the service, an old man entered the church tapping a rather large stick in front of him. A young boy was with him. It was obvious that he was visually disabled.

Pastor Chrisnel Le Lievre

The interior of Methodist Church Te Madeline.

At the completion of the service, we went over to him and asked how long he had been blind.

He responded, "Several years."

With the help of the pastor, we asked if we could take a look at his eyes. He was very willing. I happened to have a small pocket flashlight with me, and we were able to determine he had very dense, white cataracts that most likely accounted for his blindness.

A volunteer stands outside Methodist Church Te Madeline.

The view from the road in the countryside near Jérémie.

We asked if he would like to come to the eye clinic in Jérémie so we might be able to determine if an operation would help his vision. He was very agreeable to this, so arrangements were made for him to come to the clinic that next week.

Several days later at the clinic, an eye examination confirmed the diagnosis of cataracts as the cause of his blindness. We shared that surgery would be necessary to restore his vision.

A typical Haitian house in the countryside.

Later that day, he underwent successful cataract surgery with intraocular lens implantation on one of his eyes. He was placed in our overnight stay facility located just outside the clinic, where he was given a bed and fed an evening meal.

On our return to the clinic the following morning, he was brought in for his post-operative check. Upon removal of the patch and cleaning of the eyelids, he opened his eyes and a big smile erupted on his face.

He then got up from the chair, went to the door, and with an emotional display shouted, "Thank you, God! Thank you, God!"

He then threw down his stick he had been using. "I don't need this anymore!" Turning to us, he cried, "Thank you, thank you!"

After everything settled down, we gave him and the person with him instructions for his postoperative care. Arrangements were made for him to return in two weeks.

As he was leaving, Pastor Chrisnel told him to be sure and come to church the next week, as the reason his sight was restored was because both he and the doctor had attended church that Sunday.

Chapter 10

A Lady Named Catherine

When driving to the eye clinic at Gebeau early one morning, our team saw a small young girl carrying an older woman on her back toward the outside waiting area at the clinic.

As she was very near the clinic, we did not offer assistance but arranged to see her in our first group of patients.

When she arrived, she was taken to one of our examination rooms.

We learned her name was Catherine. She had diabetes and had lost use of both legs, probably because of her diabetic condition. She told us she had been blind for two years.

Examination revealed complete white cataracts in both eyes.

When we asked her daughter about their situation, we learned that carrying her mother on her back was their only mode of transportation. With a smile on her face, the daughter said she was happy to do so because she was her mother.

Our team performed successful cataract surgery with intraocular lens implantation on one eye, resulting in good visual acuity. Later, another team performed successful cataract surgery on the remaining eye.

Upon our return to the United States, we were able to obtain a wheelchair with large bicycle-type tires that could easily navigate the bumpy, uneven roads. The wheelchair was shipped to Jérémie along with our container of medical supplies the following year.

The following year, when our team arrived in Jérémie, we were able to get Ms. Catherine's address with help from the Methodist minister so we could deliver the wheelchair to her home.

Ms. Catherine lived in a small wooden frame structure with a tin roof. There we were greeted by her daughter and taken to Ms. Catherine's bedroom, which was only large enough to hold the bed in which she was lying.

We told Ms. Catherine we had a surprise for her. When we brought in the wheelchair, the smiles on both the faces of Ms. Catherine and her daughter were the biggest we had ever seen.

When we wheeled her outside for a ride, all the neighbors had gathered around.

Words cannot describe the celebration and joy we witnessed that day.

Chapter 11

A New Sound System for the Methodist Church

The Methodist church in Jérémie was in bad need of a sound system for the sanctuary. What they were using was inadequate. Poor amplification made it difficult to understand the sermon or anyone speaking in the church.

When I told this story to a good friend of mine, Jim Covington, he volunteered to help. As Jim was in this business, he was very familiar with what the church needed.

When the system was purchased, it was packaged in twelve boxes. It was our plan to fly them to Port-au-Prince and then have them transported either by truck or boat to Jérémie. Jim had good friends and connections with Eastern Airlines, who agreed to fly the containers to Port-au-Prince at no charge.

In March 1979, Jim and I flew to Haiti. When we arrived in Port-au-Prince, we were surprised to find out none of our luggage—including the twelve boxes—had arrived. We had to remain in Port-au-Prince an extra day waiting for their arrival.

When the containers arrived, Bishop Rocourt arranged to have them taken to Jérémie by boat. Jim and I then flew with Mission Aviation Fellowship to Jérémie.

All the containers arrived at the wharf in Jérémie undamaged. A truck from the Methodist Project at Gebeau then transported them to the Methodist church. There, with Jim's help, they were expertly installed for use in the sanctuary.

The following day I had surgery scheduled at the hospital, so Jim accompanied me so he could film both the hospital and some of the surgery.

However, in the middle of our second case of cataract surgery, we lost all power—including the lights. I asked Jim if he had any flashlights with him. Thankfully, he had two.

I asked him to come over to the operating table and shine both flashlights on the eye of the patient so I could complete the surgery. I told him if he fainted, I would leave him in Haiti!

Fortunately, he did a wonderful job, and the surgery was completed without complications.

Incidentally, this patient was Manno, one of our drivers at the Methodist Project at Gebeau. He ended up with excellent vision in that eye.

On the following Sunday morning, Jim and I attended services at the Methodist Church with Pastor Edward Holmes. The new sound system worked perfectly. Everyone could hear the sermon and the choir so clearly. In fact, the system still works well and is in use today.

A big thank you goes to Jim Covington for making this happen.

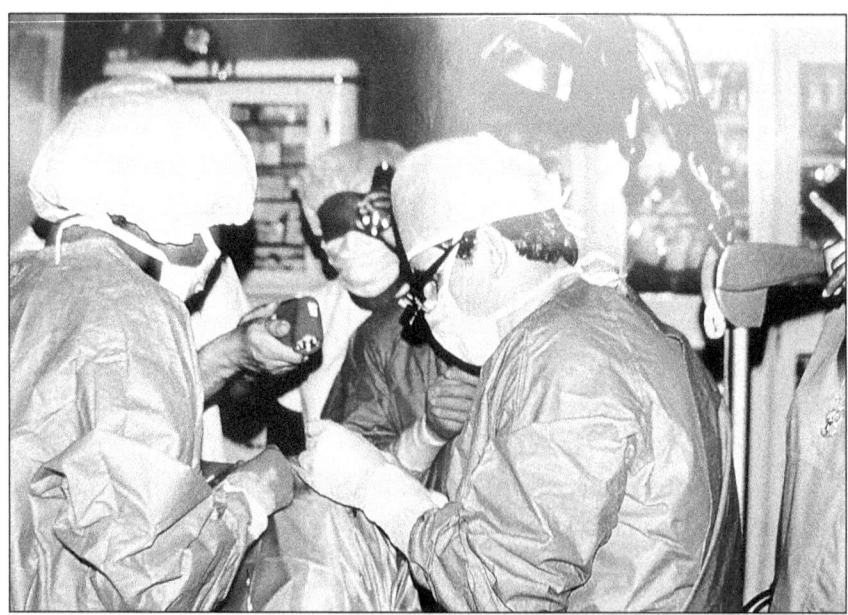

Often during cataract surgeries, we would lose power and rely on handheld flashlights (as pictured above) to finish our work.

Chapter 12

Lyse

In February 1987, our team was busy seeing patients in the eye clinic at Gebeau when a young girl was brought into the clinic by her father.

It was obvious she was visually handicapped, as she was being led by her father, holding onto one the rear hip pockets of his pants. She was a young ten-year-old child whose name was Lyse.

In talking with her father, we learned she had been blind for almost two years. He gave us no history of any injuries or serious illnesses. Examination revealed she was not able to see any of the symbols on the chart but only able to see hand movements at approximately two feet in both eyes, indicating that she was functionally and legally blind.

Further examination revealed the cornea of both eyes to be white and opaque, except for a very small rim at the periphery. It was therefore impossible to determine the condition of the eyes beyond the cornea.

It was obvious this young girl would require a corneal transplant to correct her vision problem.

At that time, the surgery was not available in Haiti because of the lack of necessary instruments and donor corneal tissue. We thus decided we would make arrangements for her to travel to the United States for this surgery.

This was discussed with her father, who was very happy something could be done to help his daughter. With the help of the Haitian ophthalmologists who worked with our program and the Methodist Church of Haiti, we were able to get a visa for both Lyse and her father, which would allow them to travel to the United States for surgery.

Upon our return to the United States, I discussed this case with Dr. Joseph Lacasio, a corneal surgeon in the Department of Ophthalmology at the University of South Carolina School of Medicine. After reviewing photographs and other pertinent information, he agreed that a corneal transplant was indicated.

Dr. Lacasio then said he would perform the surgery at no charge and would like me to assist him.

I then talked with William Ivey, the CEO of Richland Memorial Hospital. He agreed to provide her with the hospital stay and use of the surgery suite at no charge.

We then made arrangements with the Department of Pediatrics at the University of South Carolina, which also agreed to perform her preoperative evaluation and care after surgery—again, at no charge.

Travel arrangements were made for Lyse, her father, and Cecelia Mannes, who was the director of the Methodist Project in Jérémie at that time. Arrangements were made for Lyse and her father to stay at the Ronald McDonald House, a guesthouse near the hospital, during her preoperative and postoperative time. As they would need their meals provided while there, volunteers from the JOY Sunday school class from Shandon United Methodist Church in Columbia brought wonderful meals to them during their stay.

After all the preoperative evaluation and laboratory studies had been completed, surgery was scheduled. A successful corneal transplant was performed on her right eye.

The diseased cornea that was removed was sent to the pathology department at Richland Memorial Hospital, and they were unable to make any definitive diagnosis as to the etiology of her corneal disease. The tissue was then sent to the Armed Forces Institute of Pathology in Washington, D.C., for their evaluation, and they also were unable to give us any definitive diagnosis.

It was our clinical opinion that the etiology was most likely nutritional in origin.

For one month following her surgery, Lyse and her father remained at the Ronald McDonald House so the necessary medications could be administered and for her postoperative care.

We were very pleased that her postoperative recovery was uneventful with

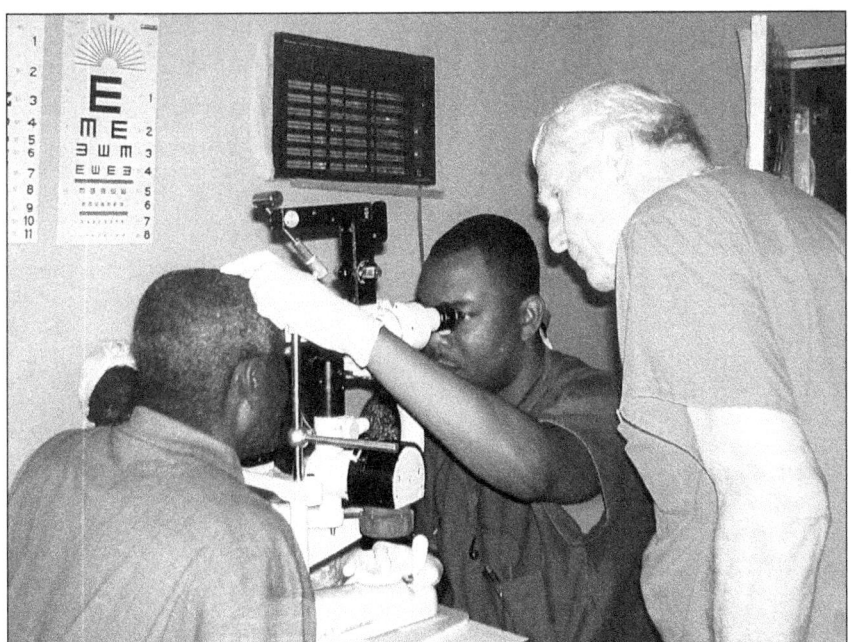

As with this patient, above, Lyse was evaluated at the clinic in Gebeau to determine the range of her eyesight. When we discovered she needed a corneal transplant to correct her vision problem, several partners stepped up to help her get the needed surgery in the United States.

no evidence of any rejection of the transplanted corneal tissue.

After one month, she and her father returned to Haiti, following which she received further postoperative eye care by Dr. Brigitte Hudicourt and Dr. Françoise Rocourt Dennery, both ophthalmologists who helped with our program in Haiti.

When the JOY Sunday school class found out Lyse's father was a carpenter, they sent him home with a box of new carpenter tools. Needless to say, he was most appreciative and overjoyed.

Lyse was followed by us for more than one year with a resulting twenty-thirty vision in the operated eye. This now allowed her to go to school and resume more of a normal life for a ten-year-old girl. Unfortunately, we were not able to get a visa to enable her return to the United States for surgery on the left eye.

After her completion of school, Lyse was able to find a job and later got married. She now has two beautiful daughters, both of whom have normal eyes. We have discussed with her the possibility of a corneal transplant for her left eye, and hopefully that will happen at some time in the future.

Each time we see Lyse when we are working in Jérémie, there is always a beautiful smile and expression of gratitude for all that was done for her by so many wonderful people to help her regain her vision, as well as her life.

Chapter 13

God Knows Our Every Need

In January 1999, our team had just arrived in Jérémie and were busy getting the clinic set up to begin our work seeing patients and performing surgery.

During our unpacking of the boxes that had been shipped prior to our arrival, we discovered some of our essential supplies for surgery were missing. Without them, there was no way we could perform eye surgery.

As we had a full surgery schedule, we were very concerned about the situation.

We decided we would make a list of all the items we needed and send it over to Sister Mary Mac at the Haitian Health Foundation, which was located nearby in Jérémie. One of our helpers had a motorcycle, so we handed him this list and asked him to take it to HHF to see if they could help us.

But before he was able to leave on the motorcycle, a truck from HHF arrived at the eye clinic with several boxes and a note from Sister Mary Mac. The note said they had found some items in the warehouse. They did not need the supplies and wanted us to have them.

When we opened the boxes, we were utterly amazed. They were filled with many items—everything that was on our list we had just written to send to Sister Mary Mac, plus more.

What was so puzzling was the fact that HHF was involved only with preventive health-type medicine along with an outpatient clinic. They had no surgical facilities, specifically none for eye surgery. Yet some of the items in the boxes were unique and related only to eye surgery!

We all looked at each other and said this had to be a miracle.

I think everyone said a silent prayer expressing thanks to God for making this happen.

Truly, God always knows our every need.

Chapter 14

The Last Surgery Case

Our team had been busy working at the eye clinic in Jérémie for two weeks, and on our last day, we were all very busy at the clinic.

As we neared the end of that day, one of our patients was a middle-aged lady who had been brought to the clinic by two Catholic nuns. They had found her in the village of Roseaux, located several miles away along the coast. She had been found on the street with her three children begging for money to buy food.

The nuns had noticed she appeared to be blind. They also learned her husband had died from tuberculosis several years earlier. She told the nuns she had gradually lost her vision over the last two years, and now she was unable to see anything.

The nuns took the children to the Catholic Haitian Health Foundation in Jérémie for their care and then brought the lady to the eye clinic for evaluation.

Our examination revealed complete white cataracts in both eyes that were causing her blindness. Our nurses, Kathy and Beth, had just finished cleaning all the equipment in the operating room, preparing everything for the next team.

After our examination, we told her that her vision loss was caused by cataracts, which could be helped with surgery. We informed her that the next eye team would arrive in four weeks, at which time we could schedule her surgery.

She began to cry and said all she wanted was to be able to see her children again.

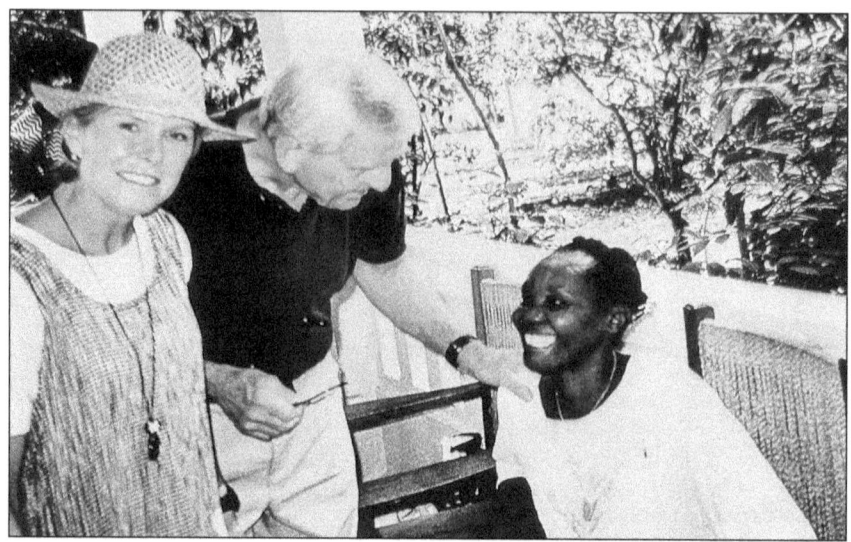

Our last surgery case, smiling after her surgery.

By then most of the staff had gathered around, and there was not a dry eye in the crowd. We all looked at each other and decided to open the surgery room and to proceed with surgery on one of her eyes that very evening.

As it was the last day for our team, the Methodist minister, Pastor Ralph Denizard, along with some of the members of the Methodist church had planned a party for the team that evening, so a phone call was made to let that we would be a little late.

When we made the decision to perform surgery, it was almost seven o'clock. After the operating room was prepared for surgery, we then proceeded with a successful cataract operation with intraocular lens implantation on one of her eyes.

After a short postoperative stay in the clinic, the nuns arranged for her to spend the night at the Haitian Health Foundation, where her children were staying.

After completing all of our duties at the clinic, we arrived back at the guesthouse around ten, but by then unfortunately the party was over.

We were scheduled to fly from Jérémie back to Port-au-Prince the following morning at ten o'clock, so we arranged for the nurses at Catholic foundation to bring the lady to the guesthouse early that morning.

When she arrived, we had her sit on the porch at the guesthouse. We carefully removed the bandage and shield, which we always used after surgery. We cleaned her eyelids with a sterile solution and pads.

Then we asked her to open her operated eye.

As she opened her eye there was a big smile. She grabbed our hands. "Thank you, thank you! Now I can see my children again!"

I don't think any of our team members will ever forget that beautiful smile on her face that morning.

Both she and the nuns were given instructions for the necessary postoperative care of the eye, and she was scheduled to see the next team upon their arrival so the other eye could have surgery.

Chapter 15

Predestination or Coincidence

While working at the eye clinic in Jérémie, it was customary for our team to attend church on Sunday morning at the Methodist church in the town. Pastor Chrisnell Lelievre was superintendent of the Jérémie district, and he had thirty-two other churches under his responsibility.

One Sunday morning the Pastor Chrisnell invited our team to accompany him to one of the other churches in the countryside, and several of our team readily accepted.

Early that Sunday morning, Kathy, Beth, Tal, and I loaded in the Land Rover with Pastor Chrisnell and departed for the village of Quartre Chemins, which was located in the mountains approximately an hour's drive from Jérémie.

After leaving the main road, we were on a narrow, bumpy, dirt road winding up the mountain. During our trip, we encountered rather heavy rains, which caused the road to be muddy and slick. The area along the way resembled a rainforest.

There were many typical Haitian houses that we saw along the way, with walls made from wood and a putty-like material and with a thatch roof. Most of these houses had fences made of wooden sticks that are stuck in the ground surrounding each house. They are called a "living fence," as the sticks will frequently begin sprouting leaves and branches. All of the yards are dirt and always very clean, with no trash or litter to be seen anywhere. It is not uncommon to see a chicken with a string tied to one leg tethered to another object in the yard.

A typical thatch-roofed house in Haiti, above.

Upon arrival at the church, there were approximately one hundred people gathered around the church, which was a simple open structure made with white stucco, mud walls, and a tin roof.

When we entered the church, we could see all age groups were represented. We especially noted all the children were very well behaved and were seated up front near the altar rail. We were all seated on one of the small wooden benches that filled the church. There were many people standing around the walls.

The sermon preached by Pastor Chrisnell was on "The Commitment to God in the New Year." It was in Creole, but he would interject English for us as the sermon went along. Several choirs sang that morning, including a young lady's choir and older ladies choir and a mixed choir. All of their voices were beautiful. We heard many hymns that morning. We all then participated in Communion.

The church service that morning lasted a little more than two hours.

Above, typical houses in Haiti are made from wood and a putty-like material.

A "living fence" often surrounds the houses.

As we were leaving the church, we saw an older Haitian lady dressed in very colorful traditional garb. She appeared to be blind and was helped along by a young girl.

With the help of the pastor, we approached her and confirmed that she was indeed blind and had been for several years. Using a hand light from in my pocket, we determined she had dense, white cataracts in both eyes.

During our trip, we encountered heavy rains, which caused the road to be muddy and slick.

As there was a good pupillary reaction, we were certain her sight could be improved with removal of the cataracts.

She was very happy to learn that she might be able to see again. Arrangements were made for a member of the church to bring her to the clinic that next week.

When we saw her at the eye clinic, examination confirmed the presence of the dense cataracts in both eyes. No other pathology was noted, although we could not examine the retina located behind the cataract. We were sure that there would be some improvement in vision with cataract surgery.

Successful cataract surgery with intraocular lens implantation was performed that day, and arrangements were made for her to spend the night in Jérémie.

The following morning, she was brought to the eye clinic by Pastor Chrisnell. When the bandage and shield covering the operated eye were removed, she gave a big smile as she said, "I can see again! Thank you, thank you!"

The roads to Jérémie can be bumpy and difficult to navigate.

Pastor Chrisnell responded by saying the reason she could see again is because both she and the doctor were in church that morning, to which she responded, "Praise God, praise God ."

Arrangements were made for her follow-up care at the clinic, and she was scheduled for surgery on her other eye by the next team.

Chapter 16

A New Methodist Church for Despagne

During the early years of the Jérémie eye program, each eye team was scheduled to provide two mobile eye clinics during their two-week stay in addition to providing care at the Jérémie clinic. These mobile clinics were planned for some of the remote villages, such as Moron, Apricots, Leon, Roseaux, Bonbon, and Despagne.

Teams would travel to these areas by all-wheel-drive vehicles on unpaved, rugged roads that in some cases resembled wide paths. The purpose of these clinics was to provide glasses, treatment for many eye diseases, and screening for eye conditions such as cataracts and glaucoma. Transportation was arranged for patients to be brought to the clinic who required further evaluation, treatment, or surgery.

On one such visit to the small village of Despagne, a team led by Dr. Charles "Chuck" Carter from Vancouver, Washington, had just completed a long day of seeing many patients. Just then, a rainstorm produced such torrential rains that travel on the narrow dirt roads became difficult and dangerous.

The only place for the team to stay was in the small Methodist church, which was not in the best physical condition. Among other problems, the roof leaked. During the night, team members found themselves moving from one area to another in an attempt to stay dry. Chuck told me they probably would have been much drier if they had stood outside!

Upon Chuck's return to his home in Vancouver, Washington, he told the story to many of his church members at the First United Methodist Church of Vancouver. He had been an active member there for most of his life.

Chuck's story was repeated throughout the church, inspiring a group to plan to build a new Methodist church for the people of Despagne. Money was raised and sent to the Methodist Church of Haiti to cover the cost of the new church.

Upon completion of the new church, a delegation from First United Methodist Church of Vancouver—including the minister, district superintendent, and members of the committee—traveled with Dr. Carter to Jérémie then on to Despagne for the dedication of the new church.

During the dedication service, a small stone with the name "First United Methodist Church of Vancouver," which was brought with them, was placed in the wall of the new church.

Chuck was a good friend who was not only an excellent ophthalmologist but also did so much for so many in his home community and elsewhere. He was a dedicated Christian who worked as a volunteer in the Jérémie eye program for many years.

Sadly, Chuck passed away in 2012. I am certain he still looks down with pride on that little church in Despagne.

Chapter 17

Crick

We first met Jean Moncriket Jose, better known as "Crick," one Sunday morning in 2003 at the Methodist Church in Jérémie.

The first sentence Crick spoke to us in English was, "I want to be your friend."

We learned that Crick and his family were active members of the Methodist church. During our visits to Jérémie, we saw him frequently and over time became friends. We learned that for twenty-five years, his father had worked in the agriculture section at the Methodist rural rehabilitation project at Gebeau.

During Crick's visits with us at the guesthouse and the clinic, we learned he strongly desired to become a doctor. We further learned that because of the high cost of medical school, he would require financial assistance to make his dream come true.

Crick was a good student and had learned English at school and in communication with the American teams while they were there. Kathy and I discussed the situation and decided that if he was accepted to medical school, we would support him financially. We set up a scholarship fund through UMVIM-SC and told him that if he continued to excel in his studies and passed the examination necessary for admission to medical school, we would help him financially.

Needless to say, Crick was so happy and most appreciative.

In 2005, Crick was accepted to medical school at the University of Quisqueya in Port-au-Prince, which was a six-year program to obtain a

Dr. Jean Moncriket Jose, or as we call him, "Crick."

Doctor of Medicine degree. Our agreement was to pay the tuition costs as well as his living expenses. We asked that he send copies of all of the tuition costs as well as his grades as he received them.

Crick spent one of his final years as an intern at the training hospital in Cap Haitian. Fortunately, he was there at the time of the major earthquake that affected Port-au-Prince in 2010.

Crick graduated in 2012 with a Doctor of Medicine degree. Kathy and I were so proud of him. Following his graduation, he spent the required one year of social service working at the Methodist medical clinic at Gebeau in Jérémie.

Between 2013 and 2016, Crick worked with different non-government organizations as medical director and physician of service. These included Doctors Without Borders and the University Hospital at Mirebalais. From 2016 to 2019, he completed a residency in emergency medicine with Doctors Without Borders at the university hospital at Mirebalais. He is now a specialist in emergency medicine with certification from the Harvard University School of Medicine.

He has a certification in humanitarian response by the Division of international Emergency Medicine, Humanitarian Programs, Department of Emergency Medicine, at Brigham and Women's Hospital in Boston, Massachusetts. He is also certified by the American College of Emergency

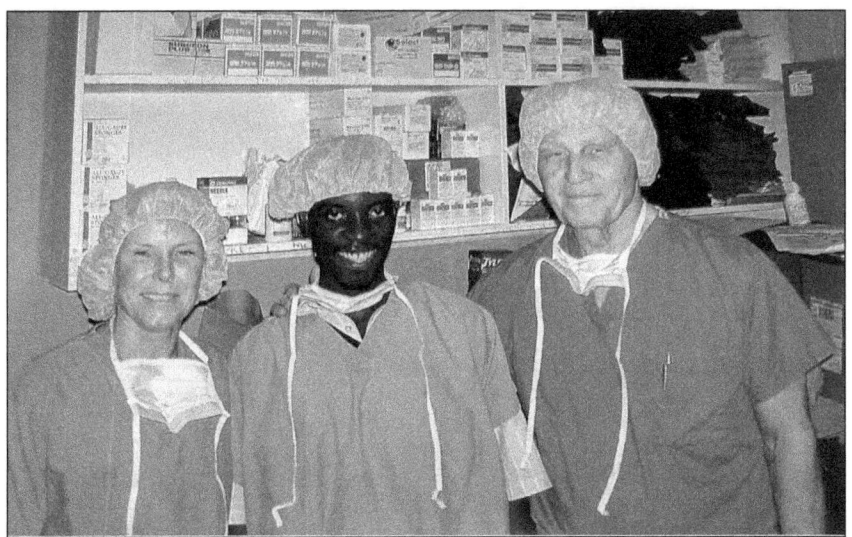

Crick with me and, above, Kathy.

Physicians in Denver, Colorado, as a trainer in World Health Organization Basic Emergency Care.

During the COVID-19 epidemic in 2020, Crick worked with the World Health Organization—Pan-American Health Organization as one of the national consultants. Recently, he took part in a medical response team following the earthquake that affected Jérémie and the Grande Anse region of Haiti in August 2021.

Crick and his wife, Cherlie Alexis Jose, who is not only a nurse but also a pastry chef.

Crick and Cherlie Alexis Jose were married in 2016, and they now have two beautiful children: Anne Christie born in 2020 and Christian Dalland born in 2023. Cherlie is not only a nurse but also a pastry chef.

Crick and his family now reside in Cap Haitian. He serves as emergency room physician at Hospital Saint Boniface (Saint Boniface Hospital Foundation), where he is senior instructor in the Comprehensive Advancement Life Support program.

Kathy and I have enjoyed a close relationship with Crick and his family over the years. They are like a part of our family. We have watched his progress through school and his accomplishments after becoming a doctor, and we are so proud of him and his beautiful family.

Chapter 18

The Earthquake of 2010

On Tuesday, January 12, 2010, at 4:53 p.m., the Port-au-Prince region of Haiti was struck by a catastrophic earthquake.

I had been busy at our Columbia, South Carolina, office seeing patients and preparing for our team's scheduled departure for Haiti early the next day. Just before five o'clock, I received a telephone call from Kathy telling me about the earthquake. I immediately turned on the television to get the latest update.

In a short time we learned a catastrophic earthquake with a magnitude of 7.2 had struck Haiti, with the epicenter located near the town of Leogane, twenty-five kilometers west of Port-au-Prince. Later on television, we witnessed massive destruction and what appeared to be total chaos.

It was obvious our team—consisting of Kathy, nurse Beth Wilkinson, optician Cheryl Burgess, Dr. Charles D. Finlay, Dr. Fulton Gasper, biomedical engineer Tal Morgan, and myself—would not be traveling to Haiti the next day as was planned.

Originally, our team had been scheduled to depart for Haiti in the early morning on Tuesday, January 12. When we had made our reservations approximately two months earlier, Tal was unable to go with us because of a problem in his schedule. But approximately one month prior to our scheduled departure, Tal had called me to let me know his plans had changed, and he was now able to travel with the team to Haiti. I then called our travel agent, Donna Bench in Norman, Oklahoma. I told Donna that Tal was now able to go with us and asked her to get him on the schedule with

The Presidential Palance in Port-au-Prince before the earthquake (above) and after (below).

the rest of the team. But thirty minutes later, I received a call back from her saying she was unable to get Tal on the flight schedule with us on Tuesday. She asked if we could change all the reservations for the team to the following day, which was Wednesday, January 13. As there was no problem with this change, all our reservations were shifted from Tuesday to Wednesday. I then advised all of our contacts and personnel in Haiti of this change.

When I first heard of the earthquake, I remembered this change in our

Haitian ruins following the earthquake of 2010.

travel plans. Our original schedule would have placed us in Port-au-Prince approximately four hours before the earthquake struck. We would all likely have been at the Methodist Guesthouse in Port-au-Prince. Also on that day, there was a meeting scheduled at the Hotel Montana for representatives of non-government organizations involved in providing aid to the people in Haiti. The meeting included three representatives from the United Methodists Committee on Overseas Relief. It is very possible that, had we arrived on Tuesday as originally scheduled, Kathy and I would have been at that meeting representing UMVIM.

During the earthquake, the Hotel Montana was completely destroyed with all floors pancaking on each other. Most of the people at the hotel were killed or seriously injured.

Only one of the UMCOR representatives survived—Jim Gulley from Denver, Colorado.

It is very difficult for me to describe the feeling we all had when we realized what could have been.

I called our travel agent, and by then Donna had heard the news. As we talked, I asked her if there had ever been a time when she had difficulty getting someone scheduled on a flight into Haiti on a certain day, as had happened when we had tried to get Tal scheduled.

She responded that she had thought about this after hearing about the

Tent City in the center of Port-au-Prince in 2012, long after the earthquake.

earthquake—for she could not remember a single time.

I am certain every member of our team said a little prayer, as did I, thanking God for taking care of us. We also thanked Tal for his change in plans, which was probably lifesaving for all of us.

This earthquake in Haiti affected approximately three million people. The death toll estimates have ranged from 220,000 to 316,000 people, which would make it one of the worst natural disasters in our planet's recorded history. Estimates are that more than three hundred thousand people were injured and more than two million instantly made homeless, thus creating a humanitarian crisis.

To further complicate the situation, it has been estimated that more than eighty percent of hospitals and health facilities in the Port-au-Prince region were destroyed or damaged in the earthquake, thus seriously compromising available emergency care. Additionally, the people who survived had trouble getting food and water because of the lack of power and infrastructure in the affected region.

I think it is important to say that almost every Haitian was affected in some way by this earthquake.

Among the buildings destroyed was the National Palace of Haiti, the home of the president. It was a beautiful white neoclassical structure located in the center of the town facing the Place L'Ouverture near the Champs de Mars.

Also destroyed was the beautiful Holy Trinity Cathedral, where original paintings like this depiction of The Last Supper had hung.

Also destroyed was the beautiful Holy Trinity Cathedral, the main cathedral of the Episcopal Diocese of Haiti in which were located original primitive art paintings, all sadly lost. These were beautiful murals depicting stories in Bible using people of Black African heritage. These murals included the Last Supper, the casting out of money changers, the temptation of our Lord, the temptation of Adam and Eve, the Crucifixion, and the Baptism of Jesus. These murals were painted by some of the best-known Haitian artists of the twentieth century including Riguard Benoit, Jasmin Joseph, Castera Bazile, Adam Leontus, Gabriel Leveque, Philomé Obin, Toussaint Auguste, and Préfète Duffaut. Our team was so fortunate to have had the opportunity to visit this cathedral and see these beautiful murals prior to 2010.

In Jérémie where our clinics are located, a four- to five-magnitude earthquake affected that region. Although there was no widespread damage, some of the older homes in the outlying areas—those made of mud, stone, and concrete—were damaged. Also, the wharf was damaged, which prevented any shipments of food and water by boat. Although there were no reported deaths in Jérémie, many people there had family who were living in Port-au-Prince who were injured or killed.

Because of the lack of medical care in the Port-au-Prince region, many

Above and below are the Catholic Cathedral ruins in Port-au-Prince after the earthquake.

people were trying to evacuate to outlying areas as best they could, seeking relief and medical care or to be with their family members. There were reports that some people walked from Port-au-Prince to Jérémie, which takes six to seven days.

Local owners of large boats went to Port-au-Prince and brought as many people as they could back to Jérémie at no charge. As the wharf in the town was damaged by the earthquake, they docked at a smaller dock

Tent City in the downtown Port-au-Prince after the earthquake.

on the outskirts of town. We were told that when the boat returned from Port-au-Prince early one morning, there was so much joy and celebration. The mayor of Jérémie said a prayer, then gave instructions to the passengers, following which someone sang, "How Great Thou Art" over the speakers that had been set up at the dock. Although the local people had very little food themselves, they brought some and gave it to the passengers as they unloaded.

This demonstrates the caring and generous nature of the Haitians, who were willing to share what little they had with those in need.

During the following days in Jérémie, there was a severe shortage of basic needs such as food, water, and fuel, as most of these items normally came from Port-au-Prince.

Many of those who came to Jérémie had injuries of varying severity requiring medical care and were taken to the hospital by any means available. To further add to the problems, the hospital had very limited supplies with which to treat the influx of patients.

As we with UMVIM-SC along with Wade McGuinn, founder of the Haiti Children Project, began receiving this information, we immediately began making plans to do what we could to help with the dire situation in Jérémie. Tim Floyd, director of marketing at Palmetto Richland Hospital, was contacted, who then contacted Rick Foster, president and CEO of the

South Carolina Hospital Association to see what they could do to help us obtain urgently needed medical supplies and medications to send to Jérémie.

In just a short period of time, they had contacted most of the hospitals in South Carolina, who donated more than one million dollars in medications and medical supplies for Haiti.

We were informed that there was no X-ray film at the hospital, so Eli Rozier from Orange Park, Florida, was contacted. Eli was a member of our UMVIM Jérémie support group and in the radiology business. He was able to obtain one thousand X-ray film donated by Kodak, which was included in the supplies being flown to Jérémie.

Wade contacted Bankair charter airlines, who allowed us to use their hanger at Columbia Metropolitan Airport, to store the donated supplies there.

Wade then made contact with Todd Meares, a contractor in Tampa, Florida, who offered to fly the supplies directly into Jérémie using his plane, which could carry up to three thousand pounds. Because of the chaotic situation in Port-au-Prince, the Haitian government granted us permission to fly these supplies directly into Jérémie.

Todd made more than a dozen flights into the small airport in Jérémie with its rocky, gravel runway.

Later, Go Ministries opened a hangar at the international airport in Santo Domingo in the Dominican Republic, which would allow storage of supplies. From there the supplies were flown into Jérémie and other areas in Haiti. UPS offered to transport the remainder of our supplies from Columbia Metropolitan Airport to the airport in Santo Domingo at no cost to us. This facilitated making for shorter flights into Jérémie.

We find it difficult to estimate how many lives were saved or how much suffering was relieved by these medications and medical supplies that were so generously donated by many of the hospitals here in South Carolina. We were so grateful for Todd Meares and his airplane for making it possible for us to be able to transport all these supplies to Jérémie.

The faith of our friends and associates within the Methodist Church of Haiti in Jérémie stayed strong during this crisis. The connections within the community that had been planted through the work of both the eye clinic and the Haiti Children Project helped us to be able to respond quickly to this dire emergency.

Chapter 19

The Present and Planned Future

No teams have been able to travel to Haiti for the past several years because of the political instability there. Increasing gang activity has resulted in widespread violence, murders, and kidnapping in that country, which grows worse each day.

It is estimated the gangs now control more than eighty percent of the capital, Port-au-Prince, thereby controlling most of the major roads in and out of the city.

This has led to an interruption in the supply chain, resulting in a shortage of vital supplies such as fuel, food, and water throughout the country, which now causes most Haitians to live in poverty and insecurity.

Because of these factors, we can no longer send our shipments of medicines and medical supplies for the Methodist clinics to Jérémie by the usual shipping routes, which go through Port-au-Prince.

Fortunately, we are now able to fly these supplies directly into the small airport in Jérémie by way of Agape Missionary Flights out of Venice, Florida, which is a Christian nonprofit organization whose mission is to fly mission supplies and mail to the Caribbean area.

All of our clinics—including the medical, dental, tuberculosis, and eye clinics in the Methodist project at Gebeau—continue to provide much-needed care for the people in the Jérémie region despite the problems in the country.

The medical clinic is staffed by two full-time physicians and the dental clinic by a full-time dentist. The eye clinic is staffed one week each month

Me (center) with Dr. Brigitte Hudicourt and Dr. Sadrac "Johnny" Marcelus. Dr. Marcelus is a well-trained ophthalmologist from Port-au-Prince who has worked with our program since 2007.

Dr. Marcelus (center) with Dr. Finlay and myself.

by Dr. Sadrac Marcelus, a well-trained ophthalmologist from Port-au-Prince who has worked with our program since 2007. He provides quality eye care and surgery for those with eye problems in that region.

Although the United Nations has approved an international force to aid Haiti in controlling the gangs, there is no way to predict when the situation will become stable and secure enough for the United States to lift the travel ban so our teams can resume travel to Jérémie to work in the clinics.

In the meantime, we will continue to support these clinics financially as well as with the shipment of medicines and supplies necessary for them to continue offering quality care for those in need in the Jérémie region.

How to Help

If you would like to help the Eye Clinic at the Methodist Project at Gebeau in Jérémie, Haiti, send a check to:

Haiti Eye Program of UMVIM-SC
c/o Conference Treasurer
South Carolina Conference of the United Methodist Church
4908 Colonial Drive
Columbia, SC 29203

If you'd like more information about volunteering or making a donation, email Dr. Hal Crosswell Jr. at hcrosswell34@yahoo.com.

About the Author

Dr. Hal H. Crosswell Jr. has been a member of the board of the United Methodist Volunteers In Mission program since its beginning, serving as coordinator of ophthalmological services in the Caribbean area.

Crosswell has practiced ophthalmology (diseases and surgery of the eye) in the Columbia, South Carolina, area at the Columbia Eye Clinic for more than fifty years.

He is a graduate of the University of South Carolina (1956) and the Medical University of South Carolina (1960). He then completed a one-year internship at Grady Memorial Hospital in Atlanta, Georgia (1961). After serving as a medical officer in the United States Air Force, Crosswell completed his residency in ophthalmology at the Emory University School of Medicine in Atlanta (1964-1967). He is a Fellow of the American Academy of Ophthalmology and the American College of Surgeons and a Diplomat of the American Board of Ophthalmology.

Crosswell served as clinical associate professor of ophthalmology on the staff of the USC School of Medicine for more than twenty years and, in 2007, was awarded the Alginon Sidney Sullivan award by the university for his work in Haiti.

He was awarded the Order of the Palmetto by the State of South Carolina in 2006.

He and his family are longtime members of Shandon United Methodist Church in Columbia.

www.ingramcontent.com/pod-product-compliance
Lightning Source LLC
Chambersburg PA
CBHW050915160426
43194CB00011B/2415